Beings of the Christ Light

SHARE

The Meaning of Christmas

MPINGO MARILYN GRIFFIN

Lion's Heart Publishing, Charlotte, North Carolina

BEINGS OF THE CHRIST LIGHT
SHARE
THE MEANING OF CHRISTMAS
MPINGO MARILYN GRIFFIN

Copyright © 2002 by Mpingo Marilyn Griffin

First Printing

LION'S HEART PUBLISHING
P.O. Box 38926
Charlotte, North Carolina
704-553-9269

All Rights Reserved under the International Copyright Union, the Pan-American Copyright Convention and under the Universal Copyright Convention. No part of this book may be reproduced or transmitted in any form or by any means, electronic or mechanical, including photocopying, recording or by any information storage and retrieval system without written permission from the author, except for the inclusion of brief quotations in a review or use in religious or spiritual study.

ISBN: 0-9677117-3-8

Cover Design by Natalie McNeish
N-Motion Design
n-mo.com

For

My loving mother,
Mabel E. Griffin

In Memory of my beloved father
Rev. Joseph L. Griffin

"Beloved One, welcome to the reading of these words. We are pleased that you have chosen this opportunity to take these words within you. Here you will find new meaning for your life or perhaps simply affirmation for what you already know to be true within your own life.

"We are here to do this work on behalf of The Christ and because of this we are here for you. Protestant, Jewish, Islamic, Hindu or any spiritual seeker, it matters not, for there is one God present within all. When we say Christ, we mean much more than the general idea that is commonly perceived within your Earth plane at present time. We want you to be prepared to perhaps broaden your understanding of that which is known as The Christ and you will find greater meaning for your life."

—*Beings of the Christ Light*

PREFACE

This is a book that will bless you if read in the early spring or the cool of December. It is a story told after a year of study and guidance from divine agents sent by God.

These beloved emissaries of God, the Beings of the Christ Light, first conveyed this story, *The Meaning of Christmas*, through me in December 1994. They told it, as part of a series of four group sessions, to people in the Los Angeles area, and simultaneously by speakerphone, to others in Berkeley, California. In these sessions, they extended an invitation for us to embrace and celebrate a deeper and more personal experience of the birth of The Christ born within us.

This book represents only a small portion of their work that took place during weekly sessions held from January 1994 through early February 1997.

At the request of the beloved Beings of the Christ Light, I now make the story available for others. Since the original telling, I have shared it only through my homemade photocopied version. Each year I continue to receive requests for copies from people that have read it and want to share it with others. The time has come to make it accessible so that many people will have the benefit of this broader understanding.

I begin with a "Prologue to the Story" In it I laid the foundation of how the story of *The Meaning of Christmas* came to be told. In this first section of the book, you will read about some of the experiences of my own spiritual unfoldment that led to my introduction to these beloved Beings of the Christ Light. I also give a general overview of the work of these beloved Light Beings. I hope that you find encouragement and celebration for your own spiritual walk.

Throughout the book, you will find this beautiful and sacred dialogue of the Beings of the Christ Light indented for easy reference. I am appreciative to have permission to use the first names of some of the participants.

It is my hope that you will find reading *The Meaning of Christmas* to be a gift that blesses your growth and spiritual unfoldment, as it continues to be for me.

Mpingo Marilyn Griffin

CONTENTS

Preface   vii

PROLOGUE
How It Came To Be Told   1

A Sixth Sense   3
    Who are the Beings of the Christ Light   4
    A Sixth Sense From God   6

Finally Listening   11
    Centered in Light and Love   12
    Opportunities for Growth   13

Awakened by the Light   21
    An Instrument of Communication   28

Light Sessions   31
    Co-Creation Through Choice   33
    Simply Choose   38
    Spiritual Mastery and Choice   40

THE STORY
The Meaning of Christmas   47

    WELCOME   49
    INTRODUCTION   51

ONE
AN OPEN MIND 55
- Purpose of Celebrating Christmas 55
- A Divine Presence 60
- A Visit with Jesus 62

TWO
PREPARING THE WAY 75
- About the Beings of the Christ Light 79
- Mission to Prepare Joseph and Mary 80
- Joseph's Parents, Teachers of Teachers .. 80
- Parents of Mary 84
- The Title Christ 85
- The Only Begotten Son 87
- God Gave Birth to Itself 88

THREE
THE BIRTH 91
- Role of Joseph's and Mary's Parents 95
- The Divine Conception 97
- Preparation of Mary and Joseph 98
- Key to Celebrating Christmas 108

FOUR
CELEBRATE THE CHRIST IN YOU 111
- Christ Is Our Divine Nature 112
- Preparing the Way for The Christ 115
- The Creation of Jesus 120
- This is the Real Meaning 121
- Choosing to Celebrate The Christ in You .. 124

AFTERWORD ON SPIRITUAL MASTERY 147

Acknowledgements 163

Prologue

How It Came To Be Told

A Sixth Sense

Many of us hear, feel, or sense the call to greater spiritual expression in our lives. We hear that call to our hearts in individual ways that are the most helpful for us to receive it. Some of us hear it, some feel it through intuition, some people are given messages through their dreams; some have visions. Others hear that still small voice, while for many people it may simply be a feeling or a knowing. It is a call to our souls beckoning us to listen and to follow.

As spiritual people, we are awaking to our mastery with a sense that there is an imperative need for us to radiate more love and light into the world. Perhaps that inner call has led you to this book, to assist you in becoming a greater beacon of light and love. Since the first Christmas when the Three Wise Men brought gifts for the Baby Jesus, we have been emulating that practice by giving gifts or doing good deeds for others. Of course, for many of us it is simply a time to rejoice that Jesus was born. This story will help you to understand that there is more that God is calling you to during this holy season and throughout the year.

The Meaning of Christmas is a story conveyed through me near the end of 1994, after an informal group of people had the opportunity of a year of study and guidance with beloved emissaries of God. We know them as the Beings of the Christ Light and oftentimes call them the Light Beings or more affectionately, simply "the Beings." After a year of exposure to their principles of spiritual mastery, hearing this story assisted us in further revealing the divine nature of our lives. It inspired each of us to have a deepened personal celebration throughout the Christmas Holy Days and every day of the year. The Beings of the Christ Light asked that I make this story available so that you may benefit from reading it and open the door to a greater celebration of the birth of The Christ within your life.

WHO ARE THE BEINGS OF THE CHRIST LIGHT?

What or who are the Beings of the Christ Light? Why did they choose me to assist them and their work? Two good questions that you may find useful to have answered before reading their narrative of *The Meaning of Christmas,* in the latter half of this book. This prologue to the story will acquaint you with their work, which is to "awaken the enlightened," as they have

PROLOGUE ❖ A SIXTH SENSE

sometimes described it. It will also give a brief account of how they began to use me as an *instrument* for their teachings.

First, I will begin with the assumption that you are neither unfamiliar nor uncomfortable with the idea that God does, indeed, send divine agents to assist us, guide us, and intervene on our behalf in unseen ways. Also, there are times that these angels, divine messengers, spiritual guides, ascended masters and other highly divine beings, who are known by various names, directly commune with us as well. Such has been the case in my life. As you read, you may find reminders of the many times and ways that God's angelic beings whisper to you and give guidance.

In 1993, when I first became aware of them, these Beings of the Christ Light announced that The Christ sent them and they explained:

> We are not exactly your direct spiritual guides. We are higher entities than guides, but not as high as The Christ, Itself. We are directed by The Christ. There is nothing between us and It.
>
> Under us are the angels and the other lesser deities. We are the guides for them. All levels of creation have guides and as such are helped to evolve, to create, and to express their highest calling as that of the will of the God Force.

THE MEANING OF CHRISTMAS

Are they? I am not an authority on delineating the celestial hierarchy, but I do know the presence of Holy Spirit and that presence which is from God. It is what I know in my heart when I am with them. You must judge who they are for yourself. It is not my aim to convince you. These are simply the experiences that led up to hearing this story of *The Meaning of Christmas*. You will find that in the conclusion of this story, the Light Beings say to us:

> Take nothing as truth simply because we have said it. You must know for yourselves, within yourselves.

❖

A SIXTH SENSE FROM GOD

What I do know is that I am probably not unlike many people. I had a pretty happy and normal childhood, enjoying, growing and learning about life. The facts that are most useful for you to know about me are ones that may remind you of the value of learning to listen and to trust that inner voice. Those facts tell of the emergence of my inner awareness and spiritual life, including what I learned when I faced three events in my life that were opportunities for my growth. Unknown by me at the time, my response to these challenges in my life signaled my readiness for God to use me in a greater way.

PROLOGUE ❖ A SIXTH SENSE

From early on, I always sensed the call of the heart, calling me to some greater expression of life. Like many people, since early childhood I clearly experienced my awareness extending beyond my five senses. You might call these experiences having a sixth sense. If you can relate to that then you may have felt like the weird one in the family, as I sometimes did. It's uncommon for people to talk about such experiences as natural occurrences. Perhaps other of my family members had similar experiences. If so, we never discuss them. I think that many of us have had these incidents as children, but with little validation, over the years we learned to ignore them or we just plain forgot.

Such experiences showed up in my life in different ways. I will tell you about some of them in plain and simple language. There is no need to attempt to cloak them in some exotic, mystical package that seems unique to me. They are not.

As early as when I was two or three years old I knew that there was a *divine* or *spiritual* presence with me. Of course, at that early age I did not call it divine, or spiritual. It was just a good, loving and comforting presence that was often near me. Whatever it was it seemed as natural in my life as my parent's love for me. I credit my loving parents, my late father, a Baptist minister and Christian mother, for introducing God as a real and living presence in my life by the example of their lives. This *presence* in my life fit perfectly along with my parents love, my family, what I was learning about God, and all the other good in my life. In later years, I would understand that this same presence was leading me to a closer relationship with God.

I also had other experiences that began in the very early years of my life and continued through my elementary school years. I think that they were even more unusual. Frequently, I would awaken from sleep long before my body would. Occasionally, but not often, I would get out of my body and wait for it to wake up. I do not recall going very far away from my room. Actually, I would not go far because I was a somewhat obedient child most of the time. So I knew when everyone else was asleep, I wasn't supposed to be moving around the house without my body! That was my reasoning as a child. More often when I had these experiences, I would find myself wide-awake, just lying in my body, waiting for it to awaken. Neither could I move my arms, legs nor turn my head. I could do nothing but wait for daylight to come and my body to awaken. It happened several times. It was with this experience that I really began to understand that I am not my body. I lived in my body and sometimes I waited for it to wake up!

Here I was in a conventional religious family, yet I was sensing and talking with my *spiritual guides* and having these out-of-body experiences in the middle of the night. At first, I was a little afraid of these nighttime happenings and a couple of mornings I quietly told my parents. I did not make a big thing of it because as a little kid I felt somewhat weird as I attempted to articulate what had happened to me.

PROLOGUE ❖ A SIXTH SENSE

They didn't get it. They responded with just kind of a pat on my head and told me that I was just dreaming.

My family was living in Denver at the time and every year we went to our family doctor for our annual shots to prevent the flu. For two or three years, we had the same ritual at the doctor's office. As soon as it was our family's turn to see the doctor, I would take off running. One year, after my father helped the doctor chase me through his office and then catch me to give me the shot, I decided to tell the doctor about my experiences. He had the same attitude as my parents. Could it have been that he did not take me seriously because of the trouble he had sticking me with that needle? Well, maybe. By then, all that I knew was that nobody took me seriously, so I stopped telling people. Having very little validation, I started discounting and ignoring my own experiences, including the divine presence that was usually with me. I ignored and sometimes even denied what was very real, natural and intuitive to me.

My life went on. As most people typically do, along the way to adulthood, I grew up learning and making mistakes. I always remained a spiritual person. By the time I reached adulthood, I became a teacher of one of the Eastern forms of meditation. This particular form of meditation attracted me because at that time its philosophy seemed to be very descriptive of my early spiritual experiences in a way that I had not heard voiced or understood in The Christian Church. I speak of the church in general, not only what I heard from my father's pulpit. Too often, I have heard religious people speak negatively of experiences similar to my own, labeling them as *occult* or *new age* and often with a negative connotation. Wisely, when growing up I did not speak about it, so I never faced direct criticism from those who held those views. Still some people do not believe that this natural and innocent *sixth sense* is from God. Fortunately, now more clergy of various faiths are sensitive to people with such experiences. They are learning to help others understand such experiences within the context of their religious teachings. This is particularly good for the many children who now have similar experiences, insights and perceptions.

For me, meditation complimented my practice of Christianity. Both together were the foundation of my spiritual development. Even with this foundation, I still often continued to ignore my inner voice. Whether or not I ignored it, that inner voice and familiar presence continued seeking my attention. Gradually, I began to listen a little more.

FINALLY LISTENING

IT TOOK A FEW KNOCKS in life to get my full attention. As I mentioned earlier, I had three major *opportunities for growth*. You might call them obstacles, challenges or life's lessons.

I had a good man in my life. Together, we toured with a group to Egypt. We journeyed high up into the King's Chamber of the Great Pyramid of Khufu, at Giza. There he proposed. He promised me that our marriage would last as long as the pyramids. Well, when we divorced, I could not compute in my mind how it was that the pyramids were still standing!

We were living in Sacramento, California at the time. From the first days of our separation, I spent a lot of time by myself doing a lot of prayer and meditation. Certainly, it is sensible to reach for the comfort that only God can give at such times. I felt led to embrace God in everything. I began acknowledging

THE MEANING OF CHRISTMAS

God in every situation and circumstance of my life. I knew that I did not want to stay in the pain or become bitter because of the separation and divorce. He was going on with his life. What good would it do for me to continue to suffer and feel bad? It was time for me to surrender fully to that inner leading that was telling me that I did not have to be in pain. So, after years of spiritual and religious reading and studying—beginning with what I had heard from my father's pulpit and other spiritual disciplines that I explored—I asked myself when was I going to start using this stuff? I thought that it was about time. It was no longer enough for me to know and love God. That was the easy part. The time was past due for me to act with the authority that God has given to all of those that claim to serve the light of God.

CENTERED IN LIGHT AND LOVE

So, I began very simply by practicing staying centered in light and love at all times. Finding myself single and starting over again, making this choice was healing for me, though not always easy because I was facing new uncertainties in my life. I was not always successful and vigilant, but the more that I consciously made that choice, everything seemed to click and work together for my highest good. Many times, it seemed that with just having a thought, my desire would manifest. I attribute this to choosing love, choosing to be in alignment with God. I was beginning to have a deeper understanding about choosing to live in the

Light and I soon had the first of three opportunities to practice this new awareness.

OPPORTUNITIES FOR GROWTH

There were times when my ex-husband and I had to meet to talk about those "marriage ending" business and money matters. You know the ones; those things that are wrapped in ribbons of stress. I decided that I would begin with him, so I surrounded him in light and love. Before his arrival at the house, I would pray for God's guidance. While in prayer, I felt God's Divine Presence moving through me and surrounding me. Before ending the prayer, I prayed that God's Presence would be with him and I visualized light and love surrounding him, as well. I don't know what this did for him, but it gave me a place of center, a place of truth, a place of being present in God from which to speak and act. It contributed to the harmony that has been the basis for our continued friendship. He is now like a close brother to me. A warm friendship extends to his lovely new wife, as well. Little did I know that this was just the warm-up for the challenges and great blessing that lie ahead.

My second opportunity for growth presented itself when I was ready to sell the house that we had lived in and then move to Los Angeles where my family lived. I did not have to put a "For Sale" sign in my front yard. People heard that my house was for sale from friends. Potential buyers dropped by or telephoned me. That is the way that I meant Ms. C., the woman that agreed to buy my house. She telephoned and told me of her interest and I invited her over for a look.

Now, this is where it gets very embarrassing, both spiritually and in fact.

I was still very much into my new relationship with God, staying centered in the light and seeing the good in everything. It seemed that for every situation presented to me, big or small, that I had divine support. Because I rightfully felt that God was in control, I let that color my objectivity. What could be wrong with God being in control? Nothing! Not as long as I did not shift my view of *God in control*, to mean that I could forgo responsibility for the things that came into my life. That included paying attention to my intuition, that inner voice of warning. This was a great lesson.

So, when Ms. C. arrived at my house, I immediately liked her. I was impressed with her positive and affirming conversation. I expected nothing less because I felt that God had sent each of the prospective buyers, including Ms. C. Nevertheless, my intuition warned me that something was not quite right. Unfortunately, I abandoned those feelings simply because she told me that she was a Christian. Added to that, without prompting from me, she offered the price that I wanted. Great! We had a deal. She explained that she used to work in a real estate office, and all that we needed was to purchase the standard contracts and draw up the forms. I thought this was a good thing, no real estate agents. We would just do it ourselves.

PROLOGUE ❖ FINALLY LISTENING

All along, God was giving me signs that there was a better way to do this, but I ignored them. I was anxious to hurry up and move and she was saying what I wanted to hear, so I ignored those inner cues. My friend, Jann, who has purchased and sold several properties on her own, advised me on the proper steps to take regarding escrow, titles, etc., but I also ignored her.

It is embarrassing to tell you that my logic was that God must have sent this woman who offered the right price, was familiar with real estate, and was a Christian! I overlooked sound business principles and God's warning to use my intelligence to properly care for and manage the blessing of this home.

"Fine. You do the paperwork and I'll just pack up and get ready to move to Los Angeles," I told her, not knowing that I was about to have an opportunity to learn a big lesson.

A day or two before I was to move, Ms. C. brought to me what would turn out to be my third opportunity for growth. She told me that there was a boarder renting a bedroom at her mother's house. She happened to be moving to Los Angeles the same weekend. The moving van she rented was full size and there was plenty of room for my things. Well, this seemed to be a godsend. The woman came over to the house with her seven-year-old granddaughter. When meeting her, I felt a warning twinge in my stomach. Well, this time I was fully cognizant of ignoring my inner voice. I decided that I would lean towards the expediency of having my things in Los Angeles instead of stored there. I changed my plans to leave my things in storage in Sacramento and decided to share the expense of the moving van.

The next day I drove to Los Angeles. When I called to inquire about my furniture, the woman had not yet arrived. Then I tried to cash the check from Ms. C., the woman who had bought my house. Her check bounced. I called her and she assured me, however, that it was just a question of money crossing accounts, not to worry. She sent me another check and it bounced.

By this time, I had been in Los Angeles for two weeks. I still did not have my furniture. I now knew and accepted that the woman with the moving van was not coming and that I would never see my things again. For a moment, the pain seemed that it would be unbearable with the realization of this loss, but in that same moment, I was aware that I had two choices of response. The first, was to feel immobilized, succumbing to grief and despair because just about everything that I owned was gone. The second choice was to choose love and forgiveness, freeing me to feel unburdened by this loss so that I could move on with my life.

Fortunately, I had continued the practice of maintaining light and love. I did not always do it perfectly or consistently, and frankly, that is the same case today. But, because what I had been practicing was in the forefront of my awareness at the time, in an instant, I was able to make a decision to love that woman. In my mind, I surrounded her with light and love, just as I had done with my ex-husband. I figured if someone needed to steal my furniture, then they needed the light and love that I was sending her way, more than I needed the possessions.

Now do not get me wrong. I was only able to do it because it was clear in my intention to choose to stay centered in God. As I said earlier, I knew it was time for me to apply what I had learned over the years. Although while struggling to make right decisions, sometimes messing up, as the saying goes, and making mistakes and errors in my choices, I continued to feel inspired to stay centered in God. I did not know for what purpose, but I was sensing a powerful call to something greater. God was certainly giving me the opportunity to answer!

In spite of Ms. C.'s bouncing checks, I continued with the same focus throughout all of my dealings with her. I was concerned for her because she was a single mother with an elementary school-aged son and told her that I was willing to work with her. We prayed together. She thought that she would soon have a way to meet her obligation. I also helped her to research possible financial solutions on her behalf. I also began acting more responsibly.

There were many times I had to be firm with her in regards to resolving the situation, but I remained committed not to act or speak out of anger. It was not going to be easy to get her to move. It became necessary to take that step when the next month and the month after, she claimed to be working out the financing, but still there was no money. You see—and here is another embarrassing point—during our initial transaction, I also made the mistake of signing over a quitclaim deed to her! She used real estate lingo to infer that the deed meant that she did not have to move. Accepting what she said as truth got me into this. I decided that I would trust my inner guidance, trust what I was hearing, sensing, feeling and knowing from God more than I believed her. It was clear to me that this quitclaim deed became a tool of her fear. I believe that the greatest hindrance was her fear of having to move because she lacked trust that God would provide for her. I recognized what it feels like to have uncertainty and circumstances change in your life. I told her that I understood her fear, but I had to do the right thing and that this time I would seek professional help. I spoke to a real estate broker who advised that because of the quitclaim deed, I should seek legal counsel, which I did.

Finally, after eight months, I did what I had to do and we went to court. The judge gave her three days to leave the house and she did. When we walked out of the courtroom, she was in tears. She embraced me and thanked me. Ms. C. was appreciative that through it all, I remained loving and always treated her with kindness and respect.

The decision to stay out of resentment and anger was well worth it. With that choice, I found that it was more important that my trust in God remain greater than any sense of anger or fear. It also taught me that it is true that you can love your adversaries. There is no need to get caught up in hate, anger, bitterness or revenge to meet with success. It was not until I heard this account of The Christmas story that I appreciated the significance of my choices.

Awakened by the Light

After two years of all of this—the divorce, the house, the loss of all of my possessions, I found myself wanting and willing to be receptive to God in a way that I had not submitted to before. With such great losses, I was pushed to pay attention and fully honor my inner voice. God now had my full attention. I was hearing the call to a deeper relationship with God—not my religion or meditation practice, but simply God.

During those previous two years, I often spent a day or so fasting. Then a couple of times I moved up to three days. Having learned how to safely fast and help rid the body of toxins, I managed to fast a full ten days. Once I settled the matter of the house with Ms. C., I decided and felt that I wanted to spend 40 days fasting and praying for God's direction in my life.

THE MEANING OF CHRISTMAS

I discovered that the significance of this period in my life was not the abstinence from food or even my talk to God in my prayers. I learned that using that time just to listen, sense and honor the presence of God was in itself revealing and transforming. About mid-way through my fast, I found myself awakened in the middle of the night. Something different then that familiar presence that I knew awakened me. This time, a magnificent, holy presence was inside and all around me. It filled the room. In my thoughts, I heard a voice address me, "beloved." No one, not even my sweet mother, ever "beloved" me before. It was not a term of endearment that I had actually ever heard anyone use. Words of comfort and reassurance of God's love for me followed it. This was when the Beings of the Christ Light began to make themselves known to me.

Feeling reverence and gratitude about what I was hearing, I sat up in my bed and was inspired to write in my journal. Then I started to have an experience of communication while writing. It was similar to a prior sixth sense experience when I was told to be careful and certain that I was only communing with the Light of The Christ, but that is for another story. In brief, I will simply say that the Beings of the Christ Light soon began to respond to my thoughts through writing. They expressed their words by gently using and moving my pen held hand on the page of my notebook. This is how our communication continued night after night. In my thoughts I would think questions or make comments. They would respond by writing through me. At first, they told me that there were three of them. Then soon afterwards a fourth joined them. That is how it began.

When I asked them why they came to me, they answered:

> Now we have chosen you because your heart is good. Even with all of your faults and errors in life; wrong choice or choices that were not for your evolution, still you remained faithful to the inner presence of the Light of The Christ. Even when you lost all your possessions you did not lose your love for God nor did you blame God. You simply took it all as a lesson in life and moved only to express your love for The Christ.
>
> You even worked to extend yourself to Ms. C. You tried to help her grow. We were impressed with your love and care for the woman who caused you so much harm. You never tried to hurt her directly and tried to forgive her. We were impressed with the act of love and belief in The Christ Presence. So it was not a loss but a great gain and you have been rewarded by this opportunity to share the love with others. You are a blessed woman and we are very pleased with you.

Shortly after they first began to communicate with me, I asked to see them since I had only perceived

THE MEANING OF CHRISTMAS

these Beings through feeling them, hearing them and reading their words. When they visibly showed themselves to me, I saw what looked like tiny particles of light, like energy, individual sparkling columns of energy. When I saw this, I remembered that I had seen similar tiny sparkling lights from time to time throughout my life.

One Sunday morning, following my meditation, I continued to feel that wonderful holy divine presence. It was the same presence and feeling that I was aware of long before I began meditating. It was the same Christ presence felt in church during prayer time and especially during the serving of communion. I soon felt the presence of the Beings of the Christ Light and was aware of their desire to speak with me. That morning, it was quite beautiful, I thought. In that message, they said:

> Mpingo, you must now be with God! Be with the only power there is. There is only God and so it is! You are now in the presence of God. God does the work and so it is. God is the power. Use it now! God is the power and the source of your life. God is all and all.
>
> God is! God is! God is! God is! God is! God is! God is! God is! God is! God is! God is! God is! God is! God is! God is! God is! God is!

> You know this Truth. Feel the power and presence of God now. You are one with God. And so it is and so it is.
>
> You are one with God!
>
> You are now in awhile going to see God in action. Believe! Believe! Believe in God! You are not believing completely. Believe. Believe, Mpingo.
>
> You must know for yourself and so it is!
>
> Good Bye!

I enjoyed the time I spent with these beloved Beings of the Christ Light. I was gaining so much from their love and wisdom. I began to ask them about my daily affairs and concerns. This was the same thing I would later see other people do with them, as well. Instead of me using them to replace God in my life, the Beings soon pointed me back to where I should keep my trust.

> Mpingo, do not get into the habit of asking us about everything. You must listen to your heart and mind. You will know what you need to know and to do soon. Trust and allow God to work through you. You must be on one spirit. You must be on one mind with God and you must give yourself to God now and let all else go and don't worry or

THE MEANING OF CHRISTMAS

be concerned about anything at all. You will be able to do a lot of good work now in your own prayer work.

For about six months, I did not tell anyone that I was having conversations with celestial beings. I did not know how or if I should. I thought that it would greatly benefit other people to hear their wisdom but I was not quite sure how I would tell anyone. I usually kept my sixth sense experiences to myself. Since that time, when recounting my reluctance to tell anyone, I have joked, "crazy people don't know that they're crazy!" What you must understand is that underneath that reluctance, I was really feeling that I did not merit receiving this love and wisdom from the beloved ones sent by The Christ. Afterall, I was still regular me. I did not think anyone else would accept that I had some special dispensation from God. As I look back at my attitude then, I find it very instructive that it was difficult to be comfortable with the idea that our Divine Creator would send these divine messengers to me. Why not to me, why not to you?

When a dear friend from Paris, was visiting in Los Angeles, I decided that I would share this with him. I figured that it was all right if it turned out not to be an experience of love and wisdom for him. He might think that all of this was crazy. I was willing to risk it with him because I knew that my friend, Thomas, would soon return to Paris. I would not have to worry about feeling embarrassed running into him. I could live with one person—who I knew of—thinking I'm crazy, especially if that person is on another continent! When we did sit down to have a session, the Light Beings again wrote through me. Then I read aloud their words to Thomas. He responded aloud with his comments or questions. That is how they continued their dialogue. Beautiful and profound teachings came through during that session. He was so intrigued, that we ended up having a session everyday for a week.

With Thomas, I began to see a pattern of the way that the Beings would work with others. For instance, when he spoke of his personal goals and the humanitarian contributions that he wanted to make to assist others, the Beings suggested to him:

> Now, be strong in your faith and make it happen by simply believing and walking your talk. But, you must also believe your talk. Talking the talk is only a symbol. It is not the thing itself. Your belief is the real thing. You are already a success. NOW, LIVE IT! You can do it if you believe. Very simple—but, requires great discipline. That is the catch!

Thomas said that he understood and that he did believe. The Beings, however, listened to the meaning behind his words. They would do this with other people, as well, and often in reference to the idea of belief. During a return trip to the United States several months later, Thomas had the same goals and desires. Although he had made little movement forward with them, he continued to say that he believed that he could accomplish these goals.

This time, in response to his statements the Beings boldly wrote in large words: **"DON'T BELIEVE IT! KNOW IT! BE IT!"**

They would later use similar approaches during encounters with other people whenever they would detect that their use of the word "belief" had very little to do with the laws of faith. They would help them to see that the demonstration of their "belief" had not moved beyond desire, wishing, or hoping, because it was not rooted in a foundation of faith.

AN INSTRUMENT OF COMMUNICATION

The Beings explained that I am not a channel, but rather, I am used as an instrument through which they communicate with others on this plane. They differentiate my experience from channeling by the fact that they have never inhabited a physical form as their own expression. They have always been only light and energy. They said that those who channel are allowing those who have inhabited physical bodies before to make use of their bodies. I do not go into a trance. It just happens through me. I liken the experience to sitting in the driver's seat of a car and the passenger reaches over to guide the steering wheel for a little while. At any moment, I can "take over the wheel."

Usually, I heard the words or received impressions of the thoughts that the Light Beings wanted to convey before they wrote them on the page of my notebook. They often encouraged me to trust and speak what I was hearing. Sometimes, I would. In different ways, they let me know what they wanted me to express for them. Sometimes I heard specific sentences, other times I saw visual images or I received a concept in my mind. The experience is very similar to what most of us have communicating with a close friend or loved one. It takes very few words, perhaps a glance or a sensing of their feelings to know their thoughts.

I did not always feel fully confident in my accuracy in conveying their words. I preferred "sitting in the back seat" observing the writing. Many times, I assumed that I knew what would come next. Sometimes I was wrong. Right or wrong, my thought would be the next word written. You see, it was still the mechanics of my body and mind that they were using with my permission. When this would occur, one of two things would happen with the incorrect word. Either they would scratch my word out and then continue with their own or if my word was close to their intention, they would continue forming and building their sentence from that word. That is why you might sometimes find some of the passages to be a little awkward.

I found that I was more comfortable in repeating aloud what I was hearing when it was something

THE MEANING OF CHRISTMAS

familiar to me. To be sure that I was correct, I would often take a very, very, long time before speaking.

That is why these Beings of the Christ Light continued using the writing as their form of communication. Besides, the writing allowed me to be sure that I was presenting their message, as they wanted it known. Later, as my confidence grew, I trusted more of what I was receiving and used the pen and paper less.

This became the same method used to assist many, many people in their spiritual growth, privately and with large gatherings of people. Soon after the sessions with Thomas, the Beings then asked that I share the experience with other people. With a little less hesitation, I called one friend and then another, until I had shared it with seven or eight people. During a session with Sibongile, a loving and spiritual friend of many years, the Beings said that they were ready to assist more people and asked that she would invite friends to share this experience. Soon, through word of mouth, these gatherings of people grew. As we met in Sibongile's home in Los Angeles, similar gatherings of people joined us simultaneously via a speakerphone in homes in Berkeley or Oakland, California. This was only the beginning.

LIGHT SESSIONS

THE WISDOM that the Beings of the Christ Light dispensed over the next three years helped many of us in our spiritual growth. People attending the sessions represented the racial, cultural and religious diversity in America. Among those who benefited from this divine assistance were those who had committed their lives to serving God. There were people with several years in spiritual study that had prayed, meditated or fasted. Some attended just because the idea of sitting with celestial beings resonated with them and it seemed quite natural. Others may have initially attended because they felt drawn there by curiosity.

For each of us, these beloved Beings served as "spiritual mirrors." They helped us to see where we had mistaken the path for the goal. Many of us from our various formal and informal religious or spiritual practices were able to recite from our Holy Scriptures and quote our religious and spiritual leaders. Our eyes began to open as they helped us to realize that we relied more on reciting the doctrines or principles and mimicking our leaders than in doing the actual spiritual work. We began to be aware of the true depth of our spiritual lives.

Although they identify themselves as Beings of the Christ Light, during this first year of public sessions, seldom did they speak specifically about Jesus or about The Christ. They desired to be of service to all in attendance, always mindful that they were speaking to people from different religious and spiritual orientations. They often use the term "God Force." They told us that they sometimes use that term because our concept of God is so limited. Even those of us who are religions and have directly perceived God through our personal spiritual experience still, in most cases, do not fully appreciate all that God is. In the beginning days of my experience with them, they explained:

> We are from the beginning as we have said before and we are from the light! That light is the God Force. It will take some time and many sessions for you really to understand that which you call God. We are to help you see beyond your limited concept of God and to be open to the fullness of what the God Force really is. We will be here to help you do that.

They were interested in assisting us in further developing our relationship with God for this served their greater mission.

> You will come to understand our mission. We are not here to gain followers, for we want none. We are not here to start a new religion, for you have your own. We are here to awaken you to your enlightenment. We are here to help you gain mastery of life. We are here to assist you in recognizing the divinity that is yours now. We are here to find those who wish to help bring greater light and love to the world.

Mission of the Beings of The Christ Light

In the beginning days, they presented the basics of spiritual mastery and helped us to understand choice, an essential principle of their teachings. We intellectually understood and acknowledged the importance of choice. It is a very popular theme today, however the Beings worked to instill the idea in us that choice is the fundamental law of creation, and it is the basic principle that governs every moment of our lives.

CO-CREATION THROUGH CHOICE

Occasionally, I was invited to Oakland, California to hold sessions in person with the people there that week after week, had so patiently participated with us

THE MEANING OF CHRISTMAS

in Los Angeles by listening over a speakerphone. At one of the Oakland sessions, the Beings of the Christ Light again gave an insightful way to look at how the co-creation process and choice relate to our spiritual growth. Even a student of theology who was present that evening gained new insight. They began with their theme for the evening.

Know yourself as co-creator

We wish to help each of you achieve mastery over your lives; each of you to know yourselves as co-creators. This is who you truly are. You create your life, as you desire. God Force has already given this gift to you. Do you understand this?

The Light Beings posed the question to everyone present. Everyone understood.

Creation is a process of choice

Now, we will continue. The God Force is a chooser. In Its ability to create, It makes choices as to how It will give forth in Its expression. Creation is not a haphazard process. It is a process of choice, of direction. Is this so?

"Yes," most of the thirty to forty people answered.

Is it not said that you are created in It's own image? Image! Imagination: a process of selected thought. Is this so? An image is a

> thought form of something in creation. Is this so?

"Yes. Yes, it is," some answered.

Gitane, a woman attending a session with the Beings for the first time said, "I understand what you said. I hear you, but I don't always experience it in the same way, you know, and to hear it intellectually and know it may not always be the same."

> Yes. Yes.
> Is this so for the others as well?

"Yes," the others answered.

The Beings continued their inquiry to the others.

> You may have an intellectual understanding of something, but not a full experience of it?

"Yes," a few more said aloud in agreement.

> This is the case.

They then directed their attention to Gitane.

> We have come to assist you in being all that you are now.

"Thank you," said Gitane.

> Yes. Now we will continue.

They then continued, addressing all present.

THE MEANING OF CHRISTMAS

"You are the co-creator of your life."

You are the co-creator of your life. Just as the God Force gives expression to all of the Creation, you too give forth expression as you believe, feel and think in your own lives.

Then they made a fundamental point:

Thought process is parallel to the Creation experience

The process is parallel to that of the Creation experience. Simply, a thought comes into form. That is how the God Force expressed Itself as Creation and that is how you find the results you now experience in your life. Understand?

Gitane asked, "From our thoughts?"

Yes, from your thoughts, your feelings, and your beliefs.

"So, it mirrors what reality we see. I see," she said. She then asked, "Right now?"

That is partially it.

"Whether I'm conscious of it or not?" she asked.

Partially, yes.

"Thank you," she said.

The Light Beings again emphasized an earlier point.

> It is what you see, feel, believe and accept as truth in your life. This is on very subtle levels. It can be a very conscious decision or it can happen in a very subtle way, as well.
>
> Any other questions from anyone on anything that we have thus far said?

"No," said another woman. She did not have a question, but this theological student visiting from Boston felt inspired to make a comment.

"I just think that your expression about the Creation experience and the way we participate in God's Creation..." she paused and searched a moment for the words and then continued. "Ah, I feel like I understand how..." again, she paused a moment in thought.

Deeply moved by this new insight, she continued, "I mean, I just have a glimmer of...a sense of what it means to participate in God's Creation as we create. I have heard *co-creation* so many times," she continued, "but I didn't know what I was participating in—like Genesis 1," she said referring to the first book in the Bible.

> Yes. What do they teach you now in your schools of theology?

"Intellectual things," she replied.

THE MEANING OF CHRISTMAS

> With this process on what we are speaking of here tonight, what do they teach?

"Well, they teach much about co-creation, actually," she began. "The concept that God and humans co-create is very much a part of theology right now. To look at how we are as humans in the world instead of looking at God inductively. So, so much of what you say is what we're taught, but there's no way to participate in that experience of what we are taught. It's words. It's not…"

> But, you do participate in it.

"Yes. Yes, that's what I'm feeling," she said of her new insight.

> We are very pleased that you are with us, beloved. Very pleased.

"I'm very pleased to be here. It has been a long series of prayers asking for some guidance."

SIMPLY CHOOSE

Soon Gitane had another concern and it presented a further opportunity to look at choice.

"Well, I'd like to experience a balance," she said. "Like peace, you know, and to know that I am creating and create the things that I want to create and not focus on the negative things or the old things, the past. You know what I am saying?" she asked rhetorically and then continued. "To change my belief system or to change a feeling when sometimes things are overwhelming in my heart, the tendency is to close down as opposed to being open and being vulnerable. What do you recommend?"

The Beings answered with such simple wisdom.

> Choose.

"Choose love?"

> Yes. You choose the other very easily. Do you not?

"Often times I'm not always as aware of anger as [I am] of love," she said. "Yes, so, I ideally want to choose love."

> So, choose.

"So, I can say that I can choose love and it will change my belief."

The Light Beings offered clarity with a simple response typical to them.

> No. Not the saying, but the choosing!

"I hear you," she said, acknowledging this simply stated truth.

THE MEANING OF CHRISTMAS

> Do you understand?

Another woman interjected, "With the choice you open up yourself to new possibilities."

Again, they offered simple clarity:

> With choice, you open yourself up to whatever you choose.

Someone else said, "So simple and so profound and so hard."

"But, you have to practice it," said another.

> But, you do, beloved, You are excellent now. It's just a matter of making different choices.

SPIRITUAL MASTERY AND CHOICE

Throughout their time with us, the Beings of the Christ Light continued to inculcate in us their basic themes. A couple of months later at a regular weekly session in Los Angeles, the Beings introduced the topic for the evening.

> We wish to go into the subject of choice. Let us look at this.
>
> We have chosen this subject because it is fundamental to life. You must now take full control of your life if mastery is what you want.

They went on to share their observations of us.

> We have found that spiritual people often need the most help in realizing who they really are. So many of you have spent so much time reading, studying, sitting at the feet of 'masters,' memorizing their every word, but you have not taken time in the effort of living this. You are often too afraid to make a mistake, too concerned with being perfect, to be like 'the master' instead of becoming a master yourselves. Spiritual students are often trapped. They trap themselves in philosophy. They trap themselves in patterning their lives after 'masters.' 'The masters' are there to awaken you, not to enslave you. The spiritual aspirant often chains him or herself to 'the master,' or to the book or to the philosophy.
> Does this apply to anyone here?

The people laughed because many there saw themselves in this description.

> We do not say stop reading, stop going to be with your 'masters' or teachers, but we do say stop giving your power over to them. Power they do not want or need. If you love your 'masters' then become

THE MEANING OF CHRISTMAS

a 'master' yourself. That is the greatest gift or offering you can give.

Now, how does one do this? By choice, that is it. Simply choosing to listen to yourself and to the truth within you; to trust that just as the knowledge is revealed to the great masters and avatars, it can be revealed to you, as well. It is constantly being revealed, you must simply listen, trust and accept that you are worthy to receive the same as they...

The Light Beings made a few other points and then continued with the evening's theme.

We want you to know that the energy, the light, is a part of you and in fact, is your divine nature. Now, we also want you to know that there should never be any 'master' placed above you in admiration. You see beloved ones, the same light, love and wisdom you love about them you now have within you.

We are of the light, but so too are you. We have wisdom, the ability to look at your auras, to look at your lives, to know that there is nothing that can be hidden. We can move in and out of this physical plane, travel to different realms of existence, all of these things; but know, beloveds, so can you in this lifetime. Now!

PROLOGUE ❖ LIGHT SESSIONS

> Now, you must make your choice as to how quickly you can achieve the mastery of your life. It is up to you.

As they often did, the Beings of the Christ Light then began to lay the foundation for achieving spiritual mastery. At different sessions they added or emphasized different points, but usually they began with the same essential guideline.

> Listen, listen, listen to yourselves.

From there they would continue.

> Trust what you know as intuition.
> Trust your instincts.
> Be your own authority.
> Yes, seek wise counsel, but make your own decisions.
> Yes, gain knowledge, absorb knowledge, but trust the truth that resonates within, as you design your life.

The Beings then offered:

> We wish to travel the galaxies with you. We wish you to have the freedom of movement within and without the body, but we wish you to master this at will. Not by happenstance or with an exceptional

> meditation, but because you so choose to travel. You start by mastering these basic elements of choice within your life. You start by accepting the guidance that you have had since birth. You start by letting go of doubts or fear.

A few months prior, when they first told me something similar, that same little Baptist girl in me wondered about this and some of my own earlier experiences. Then it occurred to me that this might be illustrative, in some instances, of how our spiritual forefathers experienced their visions and prophecies. Their testimonies tell us that they certainly established their relationship with God by listening and trusting a higher guidance.

The Light Beings continued.

> Do you follow great masters that hold on to doubt and fear? Do you find great masters that do not listen to the wisdom of their own counsel? Do you find great masters who do not listen to their own inner voice?

Without waiting for responses they continued.

> That is all elementary to the process of mastery. So many of you have spent thousands and thousands of dollars learning various meditation techniques and exercises

> to do various tricks, but yet you still do not listen to your inner voice. You still do not follow your own guidance and intuition. These are the basics.
>
> If you listen, you may save a lot of money.
>
> Yes, yes, yes. Just as the masters have cognized these techniques, you can do the same. We do not take anything away from the masters, but have come to tell you that you too are masters!
>
> You must trust and allow your own awareness to reveal this truth.

This is only a small sample of the work and a few of the basic points that the Beings of the Christ Light continued to instill in us during their three-year mission. Aware and appreciative of their own growth, those attending invited others. Before the end of the year, through only word-of-mouth, the attendance grew considerably. To accommodate the larger numbers of people, we moved the weekly sessions to a home in West Hollywood.

It is important to understand that those of us that attended the weekly sessions, including me, were fortunate that we had the opportunity to rehear these principles. In each of the following chapters, you will find some information repeated. The beloved Beings of the Christ Light repeat some information as an overview, but more importantly, as the Beings would

THE MEANING OF CHRISTMAS

often say, this repetition is so that we may take it in and "go deeper."

During a session held that first year late in November, the Beings announced that they would soon leave for a short period to be in High Holy celebrations with The Christ in the Celestial Realm. Because there was much that they wanted to share with us before their departure, they requested that we meet with them twice a week over the next two weeks. It would be a time to go deeper.

THE STORY

WELCOME

From the

Beings of the Christ Light

WELCOME. We [the Beings of the Christ Light] invite you to share in this knowledge. These are transcriptions of the sessions where we shared the meaning of Christmas.

"Much of the random and excited discussion that was held during these sessions is omitted from this book. What is here is the basic story as told over the course of four sessions. Each one is sufficient unto itself, but if read in succession you will gain greater depth of understanding. You will be blessed with this Christmas story for it is the precursor to your New Testament passages on the birth of the blessed Jesus who would be known as Jesus The Christ, Immanuel, Prince of Peace.

THE MEANING OF CHRISTMAS

"Much of what has been given in these pages may be quite new and very unfamiliar to many of you. We ask that you patiently allow us to share the full story and as we do you will find that there will not be a true conflict with your other writings and teachings. As you will discover, we take you into a new aspect of this great and most wondrous loving gift of God. You will see a new meaning to add to what you now understand. What we share here should serve to deepen your personal celebration of The Christ within you.

"The dialogue may not have the same easy flow as many written materials for it was originally presented as a conversation with those who came to hear and commune with us. Still we feel that you will benefit for having shared this experience.

"We now wish you to know about our beloved instrument, Mpingo Griffin, and the experience that blessed her life. The first of the four sessions was most profound for all in attendance. During this time, we were all blessed to have the presence of the Blessed Master and the one whom we follow, the beloved Jesus The Christ. This beloved one descended into our beloved instrument for a few brief moments and shared with those present. No transcription could equal that or give you a sense of the experience in a meaningful way. The most important element shared on that evening was the Love."

—Beings of the Christ Light

INTRODUCTION

AN UNEXPECTED GUEST blessed us at the first of these four sessions.

On the first Tuesday night in December, we gathered in a living room in a home in Venice, California, a beach town adjoining the western end of Los Angeles. The next Friday we would meet at our regular meeting place in a home in West Hollywood. In the following week on Tuesday and Friday evenings, the sessions alternated between these two locations. The attendance grew with each successive session.

Having arrived early for this evening's session, I felt led to sit with my eyes closed. The Beings asked that instead of chatting with people as they came in, that I sit in silence until they were formally ready to open the session. I did as they asked. I sat with my eyes closed, prepared with a writing pad and pen on my lap. It became clear to me why the Beings made their request, while sitting in silent communion with

THE MEANING OF CHRISTMAS

them. I sensed from their presence a feeling of holy, sacred reverence. This feeling drew me deep within to my own inner, transcendent and holy place where I commune with God.

As the people entered, they would cut short their own chitchat with each other when they noted that I was not simply sitting quietly in my chair. Taking this unspoken cue, they each sat quietly and began to center in their own way. This continued as the living room filled with people. Around 7:30 p.m., the Bay Area gathering of people joined in via the speakerphone and continued the silence with us. After several moments of silent centering, I felt a slight shift in the Beings' awareness and then with the movement of my hand holding the pen. The Light Beings wrote, "Now we will begin."

They soon began a very special session. The rest of us did not know it, but we were about to have a humanly divine experience.

In the first chapter of "The Story, The Meaning of Christmas," is recorded the events of that evening. The validity of it and everything else here, you must judge for yourself.

In the three chapters that follow, the Beings of the Christ share with us many wonderful insights to inspire us. Their thoughts of repetition were aimed to encourage us to "Go even deeper," to make the choice to have a more meaningful celebration of The Christ within us.

—mmg

"*Let go of your preconceptions...*"

ONE

An Open Mind

FIRST SESSION

AFTER A FEW MINUTES of everyone centering in silence together, the Beings of the Christ Light began the session.

> Welcome to all. Tonight we will again work, but first we will teach. Tonight we will discuss the meaning of Christmas.

PURPOSE OF CELEBRATING CHRISTMAS

> Christmas is for the purpose of celebrating the birth of The Christ consciousness. It is more than the celebration of that whom you know as Jesus. Yes, Jesus is a most high divine being. He is in fact, a great, if not the greatest avatar on this plane. However, Jesus is not simply a great

avatar. It is His receptivity of The Christ, which we celebrate.

To be born of a virgin is a very high calling. To be born of The Christ is the highest. This does not happen easily. It is due to great work and devotion.

Now, we ask you this: do you believe that Jesus is Christ?

The woman, who would host the next session on the following Friday, moved to the speakerphone.

Yes, please answer.

"This is NaNa," she said to identify her to those listening over the speakerphone in Berkeley. "My belief is that Jesus, the man, allowed Himself to be a host for The Christ."

Yes, yes, yes, yes.

The Beings of the Christ Light affirmed her statement. They then asked the others:

Is this understood?

Most answered "Yes," with the exception of one man, who said, "No,"

So, what is your understanding, beloved son?

THE STORY ❖ AN OPEN MIND

"This is B.T. I want to know if there are two personalities: Jesus on one side and Christ on the other?" he asked.

> You may see it as such for purposes of discussion, but that is not the exact way it is however. We will start from this basis.
>
> Jesus is indeed a divine being, realized God incarnate. Jesus is of the God Force, a very high being. Jesus is, in fact, the highest being of such expression as you would know on this plane.
>
> We will elaborate: Jesus is indeed the Son of God.

They then gave further counsel.

> We want you to listen closely with open minds. Let go of your preconceptions or your biblical interpretations. The Bible is indeed God's word, as is the Koran, the Veda and many other spiritual teachings, however, because of man's limited understanding the interpretations of these books are often misguided. Do not hold tight to these old understandings. They are not all wrong, just not quite accurate. If you wish to gain tonight, then be open.
>
> *Listen with an open mind*
>
> Now we will continue.

THE MEANING OF CHRISTMAS

Instead of continuing right then, they stopped. One minute passed and then another. I sensed the expansion of their feeling of reverence for this subject so endearing to them. The intensity of the expression of reverence drew me into a deeper place within my own being. My breathing slowed, as if in a deep meditation. Following that brief period of silence, through thought I heard them ask me to speak their thoughts. So, I did.

> We wish to go very deep tonight. The subject is very special, very dear to us.

Then there was more silence, but this time it was I who led the way. I was reluctant to speak on their behalf for fear that I might not do it perfectly, I waited for affirmation that I had correctly conveyed their thoughts and then I waited to hear what they wished me to further say. Although I sensed their approval, they again began writing. I then continued to read their words aloud.

Mission of Jesus

> Now, beloved ones, we will continue.
>
> Jesus—our beloved master, teacher and friend—is our most loved one and we want you to understand the fullness of His life on Earth before we discuss His celestial stature
>
> We want you to understand His mission and purpose on earth. He

> was sent to be a *way shower*, a guide, an example, to help those who wish to know the divinity of God on Earth. This is the only reason for His coming: so that God may be realized in the lives of humankind on Earth. This was His mission before taking physical form.
>
> Now, we wish to share His experience with you from His perspective.
>
> We want you to understand His life and thereby have a greater understanding of your own. Tonight we want you to see Jesus as He saw Himself, not as has been interpreted by those who saw Him.

I anticipated that the Beings would receive Jesus' message and they would pass it on to me. The Beings paused for a brief moment and then continued.

> He will speak this in His own words to you now through us.

Again, more silence.

I sensed the attention of the Beings draw deeper and more fully into Divine Presence, into Spirit. Then their attention seemed focused as I sensed them confer with each other. I had a feeling of excitement mixed with the anticipation, thinking that Jesus would use me in this way. With a feeling of great reverence and gratitude, I waited to read aloud His words that the

THE MEANING OF CHRISTMAS

Beings of the Christ Light would write. I waited, but that is not what happened.

White light and a divine presence filled my body. Pure love filled and surrounded me. The feeling was unlike anything that I have ever experienced. I felt that The Christ Itself touched me. Supreme Love filled me. A new sense of knowingness filled me. As the realization of what was happening became clearer, it was not long before tears streamed down my face.

A Divine Presence

"Oh, ... oh, ...oh. Thank you, thank you," I began to cry. "Thank you, thank you, thank you. Oh,...thank you. Thank you," I said again. "I'm just beginning to understand. I now understand this work. I thought that perhaps...but I didn't know."

The divine presence that flowed through my body simultaneously filled the room. The feeling of this divine presence was palpable. Touched by this loving presence, some of the others in the room also began softly weeping.

Although there was nothing specific announced or said, in Berkeley they were also experiencing this divine presence along with us. Over the speakerphone, we heard sobs as some of the people listening from the Bay Area also began to cry.

The Beings explained what was occurring,

> Mpingo is now experiencing the light of The Christ and she is now beginning to understand her work

> with us. She has not fully appreciated this work and its power. So, she too is receiving as you are receiving.
>
> We do not spend time with her when she is alone for she must learn to do the work without our help.

Outside of these public general sessions, my time with them was now used to assist others during private individual sessions. The Beings continued.

> It is a struggle for her, as well. There is much that she must be willing to release and let go of, and this is difficult because she does not know what will come or the glory of her life. She is now learning—as you are learning the glory of your own lives. This is not only her experience, but yours as well.

They then asked a question to all listening.

> Do you not feel the light, love and the Presence?

Most of those present felt that wonderful divine presence. The Light Beings acknowledged the affirmative responses.

> Yes. Now, we will continue.

They then made an announcement.

THE MEANING OF CHRISTMAS

> Tonight, Jesus will speak to you
> in His own words for you today.

I began to feel a different, a new presence move upon me. With it came a greater intensity of light and love. This new presence joined with my body. My breath became softer and soon I found that I scarcely inhaled or exhaled. Occasionally, my body took in a deep breath when it required oxygen. This pattern of breathing continued. It was similar to some of my deep experiences in meditation.

I began to allow my awareness to recede as I witnessed this new consciousness within me. It was soon quite evident that the presence that I was now experiencing for the first time in this way wanted to speak. This Divine Presence asked that I listen, trust and repeat what I was hearing. Before doing so, I moved the pen across the page to invite Him to write. It was not His desire, so finally, I surrendered to what I knew and felt to be the presence of Jesus.

A VISIT WITH JESUS

As I surrendered, I found that His breath became my breath. Unaccustomed to speaking with such shallow breathing, I could barely speak above a whisper. When I did speak, the register of my voice was lower than my normal speaking range. He did not write. I heard His words. I began to softly speak aloud the words of Jesus.

THE STORY ❖ AN OPEN MIND

> TONIGHT I COME TO YOU, BELOVED ONES, WITH GREAT LOVE AND JOY.
>
> TONIGHT, BELOVED ONES, I WISH TO TELL YOU OF MY LIFE ON EARTH. I WAS SENT BY THE GOD FORCE TO BE WITH YOU, TO TEACH YOU, TO SHOW YOU THE WAY. THE GOD FORCE SENT ME IN HUMAN FORM TO BE BORN OF A VIRGIN.

In my mind, I was in a state of awe, of having Jesus in my awareness in this way and of the blessing of serving as His instrument. I wondered how it came to be that I should have this great blessing, this great gift of the Spirit. My very human and old thinking patterns of unworthiness began to emerge. I wondered if I could maintain this experience. Jesus responded to my thoughts.

> MPINGO, YES, YOU CAN DO THIS.

To the others, Jesus said:

> PLEASE WAIT.

After a few moments He continued.

> PERHAPS THIS IS A LOT TO ASK. IT IS A MATTER OF FEELING WORTHY. SHE IS WORRIED THAT SHE DOES NOT KNOW THE PERSPECTIVE OF JESUS. IT IS NOT NECESSARY FOR HER TO KNOW.

THE MEANING OF CHRISTMAS

Feeling humbled by this great blessing, I reached again for my pen, hoping that He would write through me in the same way that the Beings do with me.

> WE DO NOT WISH TO WRITE. FOR MANY YEARS WE HAVE BEEN PREPARING FOR THIS EXPERIENCE, NOT ONLY WITH HER BUT ALSO WITH YOU AS WELL, BELOVED ONES.

Some may see the following passage as validation for reincarnation. Others will see it as Jesus speaking metaphorically with the people listening that evening, representative of all people, from the days he walked upon the earth to the present. Remember that the telling of this story is not only for a greater understanding about the celebration of Christmas, but to have that understanding help us grow in our spiritual mastery, our relationship with God. Trust your guidance, the way that God is speaking to you about all that you read here.[1]

❖

Jesus then continued.

---

[1] John 14: 26 — "But the Comforter, the Holy Spirit, whom my Father will send in my name will teach you everything, and remind you of everything which I will tell you." —*ANCIENT EASTERN TEXT*, George M. Lamsa's translation, *(AET)*

THE STORY ❖ AN OPEN MIND

> WE WERE SENT FROM THE LIGHT IN THE BEGINNING. IT WAS OUR PLEASURE TO BE WITH YOU AT THAT TIME, ALTHOUGH MANY OF YOU ENDURED MANY TRIALS AND TRIBULATIONS. YOU WERE BEING TAUGHT THINGS DIFFERENTLY FROM WHAT YOU GREW UP WITH, YOU SEE. THERE WERE MANY FORCES DURING THAT TIME, FORCES IN CONTROL POLITICALLY OVER YOUR LIVES USED RELIGION AS A FORM TO CONTROL YOU. SO, FOR YOU TO BE WITH US AT THAT TIME TOOK GREAT COURAGE, GREAT SACRIFICE. NOW IT TAKES JUST AS MUCH COURAGE. SAME FORCES AGAIN IN CHARGE. WE FEEL THAT YOU ARE NOW BECOMING READY TO BE BOLDER.
>
> NOW, LET'S GO BACK TO THAT TIME. YES, I, TOO, HAD MY OWN LESSONS TO LEARN. I, TOO, HAD TO LEARN TO ACCEPT THE FULLNESS OF THE CHRIST.

Shortly, following this there was a pause. Then Jesus said something quite interesting.

> I LOVED JUDAS.
>
> IF YOU COULD HAVE GIVEN HIM FORGIVENESS, PERHAPS HE WOULD NOT HAVE TAKEN HIS LIFE.
>
> HE DID HIS WORK.

THE MEANING OF CHRISTMAS

After a moment, Jesus asked everyone:

> WHAT WOULD YOU LIKE TO ASK OF ME?

Over the phone we hear a woman crying, "Beloved master?"

> YES?

Through the sobbing we hear her say, "I have...forgiveness."

> WHAT IS YOUR QUESTION, BELOVED ONE?

"Forgiveness came to me," she said through her tears.

> BELOVED ONE, FORGIVENESS HAS ALWAYS BEEN THERE. WE ARE PLEASED THAT YOU HAVE RECEIVED IT.

"Thank you."

> BELOVED ONE, THANK YOURSELF AND THE GOD WITHIN YOU.

"I will," said the woman.

THE STORY ❖ AN OPEN MIND

Another woman in the Bay Area was next to speak. "I feel the joy to be with you again. I don't even know from whence this comes. But, the tears I felt were...just to be happy to be with you, once more."

"YES."

"What is it you would have us know now and what is it you would have us do?" asked the same woman.

> TO RECEIVE WHAT WE HAVE TO GIVE YOU. SIMPLY TO DO YOUR WORK AND BE THE LIGHT.

"It has always been a desire that everyone experience your love the way I perceive it," comments another woman in Berkeley. "And it feels good to be in the presence...among others. And I thank you and I love you."

> YES.

"During my meditations I experience that image of your face and recently I was.... I felt you come into my body or in my mind" said Bruce, our host for the evening. "But when I see your image...by receiving this image now..."

> THERE IS NO SPECIFIC WAY IN WHICH THE PRESENCE IS EXPERIENCED. JUST AS NOW, THIS INSTRUMENT IS FILLED WITH LIGHT,

THE MEANING OF CHRISTMAS

> YOU TOO, CAN HAVE SUCH EXPERIENCES OR IT MAY BE YOURS TO HEAR THE CELESTIAL VOICES. DO YOU UNDERSTAND?

"Yes," said Bruce.

As the discussion went on, R. C., a woman in attendance in Venice said, "I felt Jesus' presence come in before when the Light Beings were speaking and also at various times throughout this lifetime and a lot more recently. I feel you doing work with us more recently because of the transformations that are happening on the earth plane now. And I have been wondering what we all are going to do together?...I have just been listening day by day."

> YOU WILL TRANSFORM THE PLANE. YOU WILL KNOW...NOW, YOU WANT TO KNOW WHAT SPECIFIC THINGS YOU WILL BE DOING, IS THIS SO? THIS IS YOUR QUESTION?

"That you will be doing in the next ten years and whether we will be doing it with you," she said.

> YES! YES! WHY WOULD WE SPEND THIS TIME WITH YOU, IF NOT?

"And what will it be?"

> THAT WILL WAIT. AS YOU ARE PREPARED TO KNOW, YOU WILL KNOW. YOU MUST DO YOUR WORK. HAVING

THE STORY ❖ AN OPEN MIND

> INFORMATION JUST TO HAVE INFORMATION...THAT TIME IS GONE, YOU SEE?

"Yes."

> AS YOU DO YOUR WORK, AS YOU TRUST AND STEP OUT AND ALLOW YOURSELF TO BE USED THERE WILL BE NO QUESTION ABOUT THIS. YOU WILL KNOW. OF COURSE, YES, WE WILL COMMUNICATE THIS TO YOU, BUT FROM THAT LEVEL, BELOVED. DO YOU UNDERSTAND, BELOVED, THAT THIS IS QUITE...A REALITY? IN THE CELESTIAL PLANES, THERE IS MUCH FOR US TO EXPLORE TOGETHER. THERE IS MUCH WORK FOR US TO DO ON THIS PLANE, FROM THE CELESTIAL HIGHER REALMS. DO YOU SEE, BELOVED?

She and others answered, "Yes."

After a few more comments, R. C. made another statement. "When you came in tonight I felt a different...something different then from when the Light Beings are usually with us. I don't know how to put it. Something more tangible, vibrating at a different level. I'm not sure what the distinction is about that. But it is the same thing—just like Bruce said—what I experience in my meditation, basically."

I again feel overwhelmed by this experience.

THE MEANING OF CHRISTMAS

> YOU WILL EXCUSE THAT OUR CONVERSATION IS NOT AS FLUID WITH YOU THIS FIRST TIME. WE ONLY COME WITH HER PERMISSION. DO YOU UNDERSTAND? IT IS NOT THAT SHE DOES NOT GIVE PERMISSION. SHE IS LEARNING HOW TO GIVE PERMISSION.

"The question is, how are you different from our friends, the Light Beings?" asked R.C. "I feel a difference, but I don't know what it is."

> WE WILL SAY THAT OUR PURPOSE, OUR FUNCTION, THOUGH PARALLEL, IS DIFFERENT FROM THEIRS. DO YOU SEE?

"This is B.T. We refer to you as 'you,' but you speak to us as 'we.' Are you more than one? What is the…"

> YES, THERE IS THAT WHAT YOU KNOW AS JESUS, BUT WITH JESUS THERE IS THE HOST WITH JESUS, AS WELL AS THE BEINGS. ONE THING THAT YOU WILL LEARN IS THAT WHEN WE SPEAK WE SPEAK AS ONE VOICE. WE SPEAK IN HARMONY. INDEED, WE SPEAK WITHOUT DISCORD, YOU SEE. SO, WHAT ONE SAYS, WE ALL SAY. WHAT ONE KNOWS, ALL WILL KNOW. YOU WILL UNDERSTAND THIS AS TIME GOES BY. DO YOU SEE THIS?"

"Yes," he and others answered.

> THERE IS NO NEED TO INDIVIDUALIZE 'I'. WE ARE ALL ONE. DO YOU UNDERSTAND THIS?

This reminded me of the verse, Genesis 1:26 in the *Holy Bible*, "Then God said, 'Let Us make man in *Our* image, according to Our likeness…'"

"Hello, this is B. T. again. Does higher plane mean better life?"

> NO, NOT NECESSARILY. YOU SEE, WORDS ARE VERY…

Words were a struggle. I was interfering. It seemed so easy and natural for me to be concerned about giving the responses. I was learning how to get out of the way and trust. My misguided fear of having to give the answers shifted my awareness to the shadows of the light in search of the words. Feeling the difference, I shifted my attention back to the brightness of the light, allowing this divine presence to continue to flow and speak through me. It was from there that the words flowed. I was learning more about discernment. This affirmed my understanding that we can choose to have our attention in or out of the light.

> YOU CAN RECEIVE AND EXPERIENCE ALL THAT GOD IS RIGHT HERE AND RIGHT NOW, IN THIS LIFE, YOU SEE, WITHOUT TAKING OFF THE

THE MEANING OF CHRISTMAS

> PHYSICAL FORM FOR ANOTHER SUBTLE FORM. BUT YES, WE WILL SAY THAT THERE IS NOT THE CONFUSION AND DISCORD THAT YOU EXPERIENCE HERE. WE DO NOT WISH TO GO SO MUCH INTO WHAT WE CALL THE HIGHER REALMS WITH YOU. WE WANT YOU TO MASTER WHERE YOU ARE. AS YOU MASTER WHERE YOU ARE, YOU WILL UNDERSTAND THE HIGHER REALMS BECAUSE THE LAWS ARE THE SAME... GOVERNED BY THE SAME LAWS.
>
> DO YOU UNDERSTAND THIS, B.T.?

"Yes," he answered.

> PLEASE ALLOW US TO LEAVE NOW. WE THANK YOU. TO THE BAY, WE THANK YOU FOR BEING WITH US AS WELL.

Several of the participants responded with their thanks and appreciation. One last voice is heard to say, "We love you." His beloved presence left my awareness. The Light Beings then returned.

❖

The Beings of the Christ Light continued the session.

Thank you, beloveds, we are back.

We want to thank each of you for being our instruments of light and love. We did not go deeply into the story of Jesus on this plane, however, what you received from Jesus was more than enough for tonight. Would you agree?

"Yes," answered all.

They then invited everyone to the next meeting.

Let those who are willing and ready to share this experience be with us, as well. We want to go deeper into the meaning of Christmas. Now we want to prepare you for a true Christmas celebration. So, this will be our focus.

Live your lives in peace, joy, love, light and live in freedom, freedom, freedom!

Good Bye.

TWO

PREPARING THE WAY

SECOND SESSION

After a period of silence, the Beings of the Christ Light began the session.

We wish to welcome our first time guests. Please know that it is not by accident that you are here. It is due to the call of your heart and you have heard the call. This is not for everyone. Only those who have ears that will hear the sweet voice of the God Force. So you have heard, and you have responded because this is for you who are on the path of enlightenment and wish to be full co-creators along the path. So, we welcome you.

THE MEANING OF CHRISTMAS

Tonight we wish to continue our discussion on the meaning of Christmas. We will go deep.

Now, for you coming for the first time we will give some background. We have come to assist you in your growth. We are not here simply to give you an intellectual explanation about the higher realms, nor simply for your entertainment. We are here for those who wish to take active steps in mastering their lives—not for the 'spiritual junkies.' We are here to help you to break the chains that hold you. Now, we have been on a journey with some for almost a year. We have seen them let go of most of their fear. They are doing well. Perhaps some are growing in more measurable ways in these past few months than they have in the previous ten years of studying, meditating, contemplating, reading, attending church and sitting at the feet of masters.

Is this so?

"Yes. Yes," many present responded. Some laughed because they recognized themselves.

Why is this?

[Note from the Beings of the Christ Light: There are times

[when we feel it is necessary to speak in terms that will jar the senses and create an intellectual stimulus to put all of the mind, senses and feelings on alert to receive what we wish to impart. We sometimes speak in ways that will get the full attention. Thus, we said:]

This is simply because they must work—not masturbate with intellectual knowledge. Now, it is time for intercourse and conception. It is time to give birth to the new you.

Now, we do not want to hear your stories—only your truth. Do not come here to speak on what you have heard or read—only what you know. And what we want you to understand is that you do, in fact, know.

This is the greatest task we have, to help you to realize the truth within—not without; to assist you in trusting what you know and see —not what someone else tells you. It is not true because someone else may see it.

"The greatest task is to help you realize the truth within — not without"

No matter how great they may be, no matter how spiritually high, what

> they can see, you can see! You must believe this for yourself.
>
> But we have knowledge that some of you have not yet accepted this. Some of you within the last week have run to readers.

They said this referring to psychic readers.

Is this so?

With no response to their question they continued.

> Yes! Some of you have been too afraid to listen to yourselves. You do not respect yourselves or the God Force within you. Why is it that you think that the same God Force which reveals Itself to others will not reveal Itself through you? If the sun shines on one, it will shine on all.
>
> Do you see this?

Most responded affirmatively.

> So, you must know this as your truth, but, this we cannot give to you. You must go within and get it for yourself.
>
> Now, we will push you. We will kick—if you want us to—but it is you, who must do the moving.
>
> Beloved ones, we have been through much of this before. We say

this for the benefit of those here for the first time so that you will know that you are not here to be read by us, but by yourselves. You must look to yourselves.

So, what we will do is bring you to a new way of thinking—not new to creation, but new to you. It must be new to you, for you do not use it!

ABOUT THE BEINGS OF THE CHRIST LIGHT

Now, more information about us: There are four whom most often speak. We will always speak as one mind. We never speak out of agreement with each other. That is why we say 'we.' There is no need to individualize for we are of the awareness that there is no separation. We speak as one. Not due to any indoctrination or any such *group think*. But, when we look we all see truth, so we speak in harmony.

❖

Now, tonight we will look further into the meaning of Christmas.

Now, when He was to come to this plane there was great preparation. There was much work that was done by us along with the entire celestial host. We did many ceremonies. We did much discussion and planning.

MISSION TO PREPARE JOSEPH AND MARY

We [in the celestial realm] were assigned to various levels of creation and we each had specific missions. Ours was to prepare the way for Him by preparing Mary and Joseph. We worked with both before they entered this plane. We worked with them individually, as well as their parents, and the Essenes,[2] and those in their environment that would interact with them.

They were first made aware of their mission while yet on this plane.

JOSEPH'S PARENTS-TEACHERS OF TEACHERS

We will begin by speaking of Joseph and his parents.

His parents have been great seekers of truth for many lifetimes. They were great teachers. By the lives they lived they set the example for Joseph and his brothers and

---

[2] **ESSENES**: an ancient *Jewish Sect* dwelling in the vicinity of the Dead Sea about which little is known despite much speculation. They are generally believed to be associated with the *Dead Sea Scrolls*, although some scholars question this assumption. (Hexham, Irving. *Concise Dictionary of Religion*. 2nd ed. Regent College Press. Vancouver, 1999.)

sisters. They chose to live in the Great Brotherhood of Light and were adepts. They were high in their understanding and well respected for their knowledge. They were part of a great council[3].

However, on this plane they were also part of a governing body that gave guidance to high light workers entering your plane. They were very well gifted in the art of healing and manifestation. They were known to be teachers of teachers. Even here on this plane they were seen as the greatest among those at their level.

You do not hear much about them on your plane, but that is how it should be. They are not interested in any recognition for it does not serve any purpose; however, they are well loved and well respected here

Now when the God Force wanted to bring forth greater light and love to Earth, we had great planning sessions to develop the appropriate plan of action so that the greatest impact would be felt here on Earth. So we sat with the parents of Joseph and Mary and

---

[3] Psalms 82:1 — "God has taken his place in the divine council; in the midst of the gods he holds judgment:" —*REVISED STANDARD EDITION*

others as well, and we charted the course.

This was before we conceived of the idea that Christ would incarnate as Jesus.

We felt that there should be a way in which humankind could find a relationship with God that was not so mysterious or seemed to be so separate and apart from their experience as humans. It was those Beings, who became the parents of Joseph, who felt that they could establish the proper environment to receive The Christ; thus, they chose to enter the Earth plane.

And so it was!

This was only a mere part of the preparation, for along with this decision came all of the other influences that would surround this transformation on Earth. We had to determine what cycle of the Earth's rotation would best accommodate this experience.

We also had to plan how it would be accomplished throughout your galaxy. This meant that the council governing that which you know as the solar system, etc., met to chart this out in a very strategic and scientific way. This also meant that those in charge of the comings and goings of those entering your plane on Earth had to be consulted, as well. They planned who would be present to interact with the family and friends of Joseph and Mary and their offspring, as well as those governing the Earth territories, various kingdoms, countries, etc. This also meant that we had to prepare those who would act as spiritual guides for each and every one of these—every person inhabiting the planet during this time. Of course, this is always done, for everyone is assigned one or more spiritual guides, but because The Christ was to incarnate, we began to make special preparations.

Now we want you to understand that it was not simply that God popped Jesus into Mary. No! It was much more than this. This was for the purpose of raising the light and vibrational force of the planet. So The Christ was to be received in a way that would be most beneficial. Of course, there was much more planning, and other governing bodies were consulted and did preparation, but no need to discuss all of this now.

Back to our beloved parents of the parents.

These beloved ones fellowshipped with each other here on this plane and worked as a team. So it was ideal that they took on this mission together. They left very shortly after the final preparations were made. They went separately into the world, but with full awareness. Unlike most babies, they were aware—through birth—of their mission, and remained aware. They were not involved in anything other than preparing the way. Of course, they interacted within their society as the average people of the time, but they were both born into the community of the Essenes. So this was the way in which they were easily helped to grow in this honor of giving birth to parents of Jesus.

Joseph's parents ran the school—the mystery school as you might call it—and it was into such a family Joseph was born. Joseph was raised to be a high master of great knowledge in his community and did not need to carry the title of priest or Father or Rabbi. One did their dharma, or work, but in addition, continued their spiritual studies. So Joseph was a carpenter, yes, but a very high master of spiritual truth as well.

Parents of Mary

Now, we will speak about Mary.

Mary's parents were very highly loved teachers here as well. They both sat on the council of Ascended Masters that gave title to such beings. They were foremost on this council—the highest. They were the ones that the Ascended Master stood before to be so titled. They were the ones that granted such. So when it was deemed time that The Christ be incarnated as Jesus, they chose to prepare the way for Mary.

THE TITLE CHRIST

Now, understand that Christ is a title as well as an awareness or the first expression of the God Force. That is why the highest title has the name of the highest expression of the God Force.

"Can you explain what you mean," a woman asked.

For our purposes now, we will be brief in our explanation.

Of course, we use your language and many of you come from different disciplines of understanding. Each has a different name for the same thing. We use Christ because it is common to the understanding of most.

Now, to explain. When we say 'Christ-like' or the 'highest form of the expression of God' we mean

THE MEANING OF CHRISTMAS

> this: God Force in Its purest form is unexpressed.
>
> Do you understand?

"Yes," she answered, but some others did not understand.

One man answered "No." He asked, "Can you explain?"

> Before creation, there simply is unexpressed Creation. Understand?

"Yes," the man said.

> The something comes out of where would appear to be no thing—nothingness.
>
> Now, we say that the first impulse of creation is The Christ. From It everything is made. So this is why the title and the highest expression of the God Force are the same. Is that clear?

"The first impulse of creation is The Christ"

"Yes," he said.

> The highest title and the highest expression of God are the same!

> So it was this council—headed by those who later took the form of Mary's parents—of whom we now speak. Those who became her parents were highly loved and

revered on this plane and we honor them. Now, when the time came for this preparation to receive Jesus, they chose to relinquish their post for this honor. And so they did.

You celebrate Mary and even Joseph. But, we honor their parents as the ones who prepared the way here and there. Now their story is similar to that of Joseph's parents in their preparation as children growing up in the same community. So they were taught the 'mysteries' and they prepared their offspring.

THE ONLY BEGOTTEN SON

Now, we will move to the blessed birth.

Jesus, Sweet, Beloved One. To tell you of His birth is quite a great pleasure. We will begin by discussing who Jesus was on this plane. Again, he was not simply a child born of a virgin. No, he was much more. He was, in fact, the Son of God Force. We will explain.

God Force is the source of all creation—all that ever was and ever will be. It is all there is. There is nothing else but It. God Force is the life you live. It is the very breath you take, there is no thing that is not It. Now, when It chooses to express, It does so as It chooses. Now this too, is complicated, but for now, we will keep it very elementary.

GOD GAVE BIRTH TO ITSELF

As It took on form, It became a Son unto Itself. It gave birth to Itself as a Son. This is the first born and the only begotten Son of Itself and of all. It gave Itself to Itself. Now, this was in the beginning before there was Adam on your plane, as your story goes. When the Son took form, It took the form of pure love.

We won't give Its whole etymology now.

We will skip ahead to when the decision was made for the expression of Christ on Earth. This was when we decided to give the world Jesus.

This is how it began.

The God Force wanted to speed the progress of the Earth plane. It wanted to have the humans take on the Divine role that they were meant to live. So instead of humans continuing slowly to stumble in the dark, it was decided that a way shower would be sent. But, this way shower would be more than a guide. It would be the embodiment of the goal itself. And the only way to do it was to send the embodiment of The Christ Itself through a human form. And this was the duty and blessing of the Son Itself to send Itself into the world.

So, the Son sent Itself as Jesus and thus, we made preparations for It to enter the world. That is how it all began.

We feel this is enough for this evening. At the next session, we will discuss the birth and His place on this plane as the Son of God, born of a virgin. You should now understand that we are here for a higher calling than to inspire. Now is the time to do the work and 'be.' You are blessed, beloved ones. Now, know this. And so it is!

We say to you, beloved ones: Live your lives in freedom. Live your lives in peace. Live your lives in love. Live your lives in the light. Live your lives as The Christ.

Good Bye.

THREE

The Birth

THIRD SESSION

We are pleased so many are again with us. We welcome those who are here for the first time. We greet you in the name of Christ.

We will go further into the preparation of the birth of Jesus. This will enable you to understand the true meaning of Jesus and Christmas, and this will help you to understand your significance in this life. You will know better who you are as light workers and spiritual beings.

Now we want you to recap for the new people what was discussed—and do this for your own understanding. Who feels ready to do this?

THE MEANING OF CHRISTMAS

"I do." Over the speakerphone is heard the voice of a woman. She is in a living room in Berkeley listening with others.

Who speaks?

"This is Gitane."

Yes, beloved.

"What I know is that Jesus was born from a greater picture than the Virgin. He was the birth of Creation. And God was…was to be a representation, an example for the connection of human spirit. It was planned by a series of people, councils—as far back as his grandparents—that participated in preparing everything that would be in line for all of us here.…Where it began is…God is the highest force of creation that we have the pleasure to experience, to know…"

It is Creation Itself.

"It is Creation Itself," she repeated.

It is everything.

"Everything. And we, uh … can you wait for a second?" She paused for a few moments and then asked, "God is Creation Itself and Creation gave birth to Itself?"

Yes, yes.

"And the parents and the grandparents were all in agreement," Gitane continued. "They had a Council with a group of people to prepare for the birth of Jesus in human form. And the purpose, I understand, is that God had to give everyone an opportunity to 'non-separate'…but be love and free will…and I think that's all I want to say," concluded Gitane.

> You have a good basis. Anyone else?

"I will," said Myrna, another woman seated among those in Los Angeles.

"Some of the things that I remember is that The Christ was the first manifestation of God Force and—it's interesting as I am trying to remember without my notes.

"In terms of the birth of the man, Jesus… there was much discussion in the Celestial Realm as to how we humans could have a closer relationship with God. How we could come to know and live our divinity."

Myrna continued with what she remembered. "Apparently this went on for quite a while. Then it was decided that The Christ would become manifest in human form and ultimately that became Jesus. There was a council in the Celestial Realm that started the preparation as far back as Mary's and Joseph's parents. And they prepared them, to prepare Mary and Joseph, for the birth of The Christ in human form as Jesus.

"I remember a particular discussion about the purpose of The Christ being born as Jesus. It was to show us the way, to show us the way to our God-Self.

THE MEANING OF CHRISTMAS

That was his mission in being born. That's all I want to say at the moment," she concluded.

Good. Good, beloved.

So, we wish to add to this. It is important to note that it was the God Force, Itself, who chose to have more light enter your plane. This is where it began—not with the high councils, but the God Force Itself. God gave birth to Itself and named Itself Son. It was mother, father to Itself.

Now when the desire of this impulse began, it became a new birth into creation. This birth was The Christ. This was well before Jesus. Christ was in the beginning, has always been, and shall ever be.

Now, Christ is that which took part of Itself and turned Itself into flesh as Jesus. Jesus was made from It, but was not It. Jesus was made in Its image and received It in His flesh. Jesus was the embodiment of It. Jesus was the temple in which It resides. Jesus was that which became the Divine and the example, the way shower for you.

The Significance To Your Life

Now, what is the significance of this to your life? The significance is this: Jesus is that which you can be as well. Jesus was born of woman, as were you. Jesus was not sent to be a unique being, but as an example.

Now, we will go back to the pre-birth time.

Jesus was a mere idea when the desire for Christ to be realized on Earth came into being. There was not an entity as such known as Jesus, Esau—only the idea.

Now, when we had our great councils— to discuss the best way to bring greater light and love into the world—we decided upon the birth of a child as the best way in which humankind could identify with the light and love of God within their own lives. So, we set out to develop the best vehicle to receive the Son into the world. That vehicle had to be created from ideal parents; thus, the parents were sent from here [celestial realm].

Role of Joseph's and Mary's Parents

The parents were among these planes, this level of creation and were sent to prepare the way; along with their parents, also from this plane. As we told you, the parents of the parents were among the highest—were, in fact, the highest at their level. They chose to prepare the way for Joseph and Mary.

When we speak of this time…it brings us back to that time and we

THE MEANING OF CHRISTMAS

feel so much love and admiration for them. There was great joy in the heavens, great celebration. This was a time of great transformation, great celebration throughout the whole celestial realm. Every level of creation rejoiced in this event, for it was a time of great joyful sacrifice. For those who sat at the head of the councils chose lovingly to give up their great posts to enter your planet to prepare the way for the entrance of The Christ—for that whom you knew as Jesus.

Oh, Blessed be thou that gives such great sacrifice, such great love. You honor Mary and Joseph but it is these whom we honor, those who went before as parents.

Now, you may ask their names, but their names are unimportant. You need not another to worship. No. You'd do well to worship the God within you, beloved ones.

So, we speak now in praise of this time, in praise of the birth of The Christ on Earth. But know, beloved ones, that even at this time—which you celebrate as the birth of Jesus The Christ—that The Christ Itself did not yet make Its appearance. For even Jesus entered this earthly plane to prepare the way to receive The Christ. And we must clear up some misunderstanding for you here. This time (of year) in which you celebrate was not, in fact, the time that this whom you knew as Jesus entered the Earth. No, it was at another time. But, beloved ones, this is a very high holy period throughout all of the celestial realms. It is fitting—yes, it is fitting that His birth is celebrated at this time. Now, Jesus is, in fact, the embodiment of The Christ, but he too had to prepare himself. But, again, back to the pre-birth time.

THE DIVINE CONCEPTION

Jesus, before entering your plane, was first conceived on this plane and was made into an entity here as Divine Idea. It was here where the Son first entered Jesus, the spiritual being. Now, Jesus was the receiver of the Son, The Christ. Now, this was the first birth. It took place on this plane and then He was sent as a baby onto your plane but did not enter with the fullness of Christ. Only with that which would be made ready to receive It.

Now, Jesus was, in fact, born of a virgin. Do not think this impossible for with Divine Mind all is possible. And this gift was not bestowed upon a girl without sin, for that is not so unusual to live a life free of so-called sin. This gift was given to a child whose life mission was for this purpose. This was part of her preparation here on this plane [Celestial Realms] and there on yours.

Now, you must not make any mistake in your understanding of the virgin birth. Do not feel that this is simple folklore, for it is not. This is a fact. Mary, as a virgin, gave birth to Jesus.

'How could this be?' may be your question. Very simple, it was the choice of the God Force.

Now God Force, being the Creator of all life, can create as It so desires. Just as It can heal the ill; raise the dead; straighten the crippled arm; give sight to the blind—It is no task for It to implant Itself into a virgin!

Now, if the virgin has the mind of God, and realized herself to be One with God, then she is ready to receive such a blessing. So, tonight we say to you that this is so. But, we will go further and explain more.

PREPARATION OF MARY AND JOSEPH

Mary, in fact, was impregnated on this side before entering your plane. She was born with child. There was no other possibility for her. Now when coming to this plane she did not have complete memory of this, but she always knew of her connection with God and had awareness of angels and spiritual guides around her. She was guided by her parents—even Joseph's parents, all who were the high teachers of her village. So, she led a life in preparation of being in full service to God. She knew of no other life and desired only this.

Now, Mary, when she became of age, shortly after the onset of her cycle, went into preparation with the women of the *Essenes* and they taught her the spiritual values of womanhood. She was prepared in the way of woman, wife and mother. She was taught how to care for herself, her future husband and children. She was made ready for this life, as were all the young girls of her time. But she was given special instructions reserved only for her, as directed by the guiding forces of this plane—guiding the preparation for the Baby Jesus.

She was instructed in high ceremonial ways. She was given instruction in how to teach a special child. She was also told when and what signs to watch to be ready for the birth. This was to prepare her for receiving the guidance of the angels.

THE MEANING OF CHRISTMAS

Now, we also went ahead of her to prepare her for the husband. We went first to Joseph so that he might be ready to receive the angels. We spoke with him through dreams and intuition. We also spoke through his teachers there on your plane and he was also guided in his preparation as a man, father, and husband.

So, this happened over several years.

Thus, they were both prepared when the angels appeared to tell them the time was at hand. They soon married and set out about in preparation for the Baby Jesus. They knew that the time would not be easy, but that all of their needs would be met; and they knew that the child would be born to redeem the world; and they were glad for this.

Their parents had prepared them and given them the foundation to be the parents to guide such a child, in such a time. They were faced with political opposition based upon fear, lack and limitation. The environment would not be conducive to openly receiving such a child.

But, such was our plan—that light be born into darkness. For who would see the light born into the noonday sun? So, we chose the conditions of the world in which Jesus was born so that His light would be seen by those yet in darkness, who recognized the darkness and longed for light. Many live in darkness, but do not see it as such. Many live in dim light, and feel they have it all, but they do not know what it means to live in the fullness of the Light of Christ. So, Christ was born into a time when His light could shine easily above all others, and this is why we took such care to plan his entrance on Earth.

So we have the birth of the Baby Jesus, which prepared the way for The Christ. And when this most precious child was born, we all rejoiced and sang Its praise for The Christ would give greatly to the world.

And then when that whom you know as Jesus was given to become a man, The Christ entered into ITS FULLNESS! This is when The Christ entered in all Its glory; the Baby Jesus, born of a virgin, was that which received The Christ. But, as a baby, it did not receive It fully—not yet. It was the highest of the highest on this plane, but at birth, not in Its full glory.

Does this lessen His importance? Certainly not. We want you to understand the full story, that Jesus was sent to bring light into the world and did so. The Christ was and always has been. Even before that whom you know as Jesus, there was Christ.

Christ was sent by God Force into the world—not only Jesus. But Jesus was that who received The Christ for the world.

Understand?

Christ is the only begotten Son of God made manifest as Jesus. In the beginning of creation was The Christ, and from that came all else, including Jesus.

Questions?

A man asked, "Where does the Holy Spirit come in?"

The Holy Spirit would be liken unto the breath or that which gives power. We will give a complete discourse on the Holy Spirit at another time. Perhaps Easter, so that you will understand, from our perspective, the Crucifixion.

Now, questions?

A woman in Berkeley had a question. She was heard over the speakerphone. "What was meant by sin, referring to Mary, when you talked about Jesus being born of a virgin?"

> Yes, what did you understand us to say?

"Well, I'm going to read what I've got here. You were speaking about a child, a female child."

> Yes.

"Without sin." she said

They responded with a request.

> No. Repeat what you understand.

"It begins with 'the gift will not be bestowed upon any girl without sin.' I didn't understand that."

> Yes, we will explain. It was not simply that Mary was chosen because she was without sin. No.

"But the question is what is 'without sin,' what is sin? I don't understand?"

> Yes. Many children can be raised in such a way not to commit sin or what you may call error,[4] but this alone did not qualify her to be the mother of the Baby Jesus, not that alone. She was much more than this. Understand, beloved?

---

[4] The word sin, from the Greek lexicon, based on Thayer's and Smith's Bible Dictionary, defines sin as; 1)to be without a share in, 2) to miss this mark, 3) to error, be mistaken.

THE MEANING OF CHRISTMAS

"Yes, I understand."
"Beloved Beings?" asked another woman.

>Yes, beloved.

"Where much confusion arises there is often times that we are taught that the sexual act is a sin. So, many times this is interpreted when we say 'the girl is without sin' there is that confusion about the sexual act being sin," said the same woman.

>No, we are not limiting it to the sexual act. There was no sexual act, taking place.
>Question?

"Yes. What time exactly did Jesus receive Christ?" asked a man.

>This happened as the boy grew up. He was being prepared to receive The Christ along the way. As a child, he was one who all knew was to be The Christ, but he was much like the acorn. The oak was there—The Christ was there, but had not yet reached full maturity. As you note, although he did teaching as a boy, [he did not] perform what you would call miracles at that young age—as one sign. Understand?
>It was in the later years not covered or discussed in your Bible that he appeared again as a man, he

appeared as The Christ. Is this not so?

"Yes. Yes."
"Excuse me."

Yes, beloved?

"Some people assume that...well, I was told that he grew up to the age of twelve when he was working with his dad as a carpenter."

Yes.

"And then he disappeared and he reappeared when he was thirty—within this time, is that when he received Christ. I don't know if that is true. Can you elaborate on this?"

We can, but we will not in full detail at this time. But yes, we will say that during these so-called missing years—or the years that you missed—he was growing into the fullness of Christhood. Understand, beloved?

"Yes."

And these things will all be revealed. Not only through us, but you will discover this on your plane, for it is written somewhere and this, all should know.

Question?

THE MEANING OF CHRISTMAS

"Why do we celebrate The Christ in this time period?"

> Why would you not? But, why this time in particular?

"Yes."

> Yes, yes, yes, yes, yes. For us, even on our plane, this time of the rotation of the celestial bodies has always been a very high holy period, for it is designed as such. As many of you know, after this next meeting we will be gone for a period of time. This is our time to be with The Christ. During this time, we are in High Holy celebration with The Christ and with those, which you would call, ascended masters, with angels, spiritual deities and guides. During this time, beloved ones, we will assist others in their ascension, for all of creation is in the process of growth.
> Question? Yes, beloved?

"Were there not any other people before Jesus and after Jesus who received The Christ Light?"

> This is a very good question. Yes, there have been others who have received The Christ Light since the birth of Jesus.

"Not before?"

>Before and since, but none who have reached this highest degree. Each of you has received and receives now, some aspects of The Christ Light. If you have awareness of your oneness with God, you have the Light of Christ within you.
>
>But remember, beloved ones, God gave birth to Itself as Its own Son. It was this special manifested part of The Christ which gave of Itself in form through the one you know as Jesus.
>
>Jesus as The Christ transformed the understanding of the world so that those in the world would know that the life of The Christ could be found within. This was Its great mission to impact the world, to raise the light in the world. Now, after the light was introduced into the world through Jesus, it was then your responsibility to receive It—your choice—and even how It was interpreted and accepted. Thus, man's choice has given both clarity and confusion; some due to the level of awareness; some due to the desire to control others; some due to fear; some due to love. Both clarity and confusion have resulted in much limitation.

THE MEANING OF CHRISTMAS

KEY TO CELEBRATING CHRISTMAS

"Celebrate The Christ within you"

We say to you that the birth of Jesus is to be celebrated. And know, beloved, as The Christ was revealed in the life of Jesus, It can be revealed in your life as well. For Jesus came as a way shower to tell you that God is not far off, but within you. Just as God is within Jesus, God Force resides within you. The greatest way to celebrate Christmas is to celebrate The Christ within you.

Know, beloveds, that Jesus is your brother, your friend, your way shower and as such beckons to you to find Christ where He found It— within. This does not mean that you do not worship God, but it means that you may find an even greater reverence for God within your own life. Know that where you are, God is. God has created all there is. Right where you sit is the seat of God. Treat yourself, and everyone you meet with this reverence, and God's light will be revealed in greater fullness on Earth.

Celebrate the real Christ, the essence of creation, that from which all life flows. Celebrate what the God Force truly gave to the world— Itself as Jesus and even as you. For God, in fact, made you, that is reason enough to celebrate.

God loves you, for He gave His only begotten Son. He gave Himself to the world as His son. He and the Son are one. Do you see the meaning of the word of Christ when spoken through Jesus saying, 'I and the Father are One'? There is only the One, for that is all there is.

On Friday we will conclude our discussion of the meaning of Christmas. It will begin The Christmas celebration. This will also be a time to do some deep work. Come in reverence. Come to worship The Christ. And so it is.

Live your lives in freedom, peace, joy, love, and in the light. Live in the light of The Christ.

Good Bye.

"*It is not enough to celebrate the birth of the Baby Jesus. Celebrate the revelation of The Christ in you...*"

FOUR

CELEBRATE THE CHRIST IN YOU

FOURTH SESSION

WE ARE PLEASED to have you all with us. Again, we will give a brief overview of our work.

We have helped many to know and accept full responsibility for their lives; to know that everything in their lives is their choice. EVERYTHING! For you who are not familiar with the principles of divine law, this may be difficult for you to accept, but we say to you, choose to be patient with yourselves. You will understand this law, as you are receptive to the light.

Choice is a divine law

THE MEANING OF CHRISTMAS

CHRIST IS OUR DIVINE NATURE

Tonight we will not spend much time on these basic principles. We wish to conclude our discussion of the meaning of Christmas. Tonight we wish you to understand Jesus and The Christ. They are not the same, but they are of the same source and serve the same purpose.

We wish to give greater understanding of that which we call The Christ as your own divine nature. This is, in fact, your true self. You are, in fact, The Christ unrealized. This is why we have come, and why others like us are now being sent throughout your plane to bring about greater realization of this truth. We are here to usher in the transformation of your plane. We are here to help light workers, such as yourselves to step out and claim the fullness of The Christ within you.

We want you to get beyond your metaphysical and religious understanding of this idea. It is time to be It. Stop hiding behind your books and memorization of Bible verses. Know, beloved ones, that the word is as equally available to you as it was to the ancient ones. The truth did not stop when the Bible was written. The truth is not available only to a few. You must know that you, beloved ones, are just as capable of receiving truth and light and you must simply choose to do so.

We want you to turn away from your fear. Turn away from being solely dependent upon what the Bible[5] says, what your guru says, what your minister says. Stop using them as crutches. Learn to hear and feel what God says directly to you. If God will speak through the Bible, your gurus, your teachers, God will and does speak to you as well. Your job is to trust what you hear within. Do not use your teachers to hide behind or merely as your 'feel good' pill for the week. You must learn beloved ones, that yes, it is God speaking directly to you.

Hear and feel what God says directly to you

Do you have to ask someone else, 'Is that God I hear?' No! Only ask yourselves, beloved ones. This is what your gurus, ministers and teachers have done. They have learned to listen and trust for

---

[5]John 5:39-40, 42,44 — "You search the Scriptures, because you think that in them you have eternal life; and it is these that bear witness of Me; and you are unwilling to come to Me, that you may have life....but, I know you, that you do not have the love of God in yourselves. "How can you believe, when you receive glory from one another, and you do not seek the glory that is from the one and only God?" —*NEW AMERICAN STANDARD BIBLE, (NASB)*

themselves. Yes, they have studied and read, but not for the sake of knowing. They did their own inner work to know for themselves. Is this not so, Rev. Dunn?

"Yes," responded Rev. Juanita Dunn, a well respected minister visiting for the first time.

Yes, yes. Neither the books nor the teachers could give it to them, nor could a certificate or a diploma. This is only a symbol of inner work. The knowing is not in the diploma. The knowing is within the person's mind and awareness, as well as their heart, their very Being. It is within their very breath. This too is so, is it not, Rev. Dunn?

"Yes."

You cannot know it for them. You can know it for you. You can see the truth of their lives only from knowing the truth of your own. Is this so?

"This is so."

You will better understand, tonight, The Christ within you. And, if you choose it, you can know The Christ for yourself, just as those here who have done their inner work."

PREPARING THE WAY FOR THE CHRIST

We will begin tonight's lesson.

Tonight we will continue our discussion on the preparation on [our] plane for the appearance of The Christ on Earth. We will review for those with us for the first time.

When we speak of this beautiful subject, we feel so deep in the light. We have such great fullness. To speak of this time is such a great pleasure, so delightful. We feel to be silent, but for most, it would be too difficult to hear. So, we speak softly, for the most part.

We have said previously that there was much preparation on this plane. We prepared the way on all levels of creation. We had many planning discussions once the God Force made known Its desire to bring greater light and love to your plane. As we said previously, we had all those in charge of every aspect of creation prepare the way: those in charge of the functioning of the universal bodies; those in charge of the great masters; those in charge of giving direction to spiritual guides; those in charge of the comings and goings in and out of your plane in human form, as well as ethereal form; those who sat at the heads of the great commissions, all participated to name only a few.

THE MEANING OF CHRISTMAS

Everything worked within this framework for the manifestation of the fullness of The Christ in human form.

As we've said, The Christ is both an awareness as the finest impulse of creation from which all else in creation flows, as well as the highest title given to the highest master. This is what Jesus gained while here on earth, the title The Christ. He was not born Christ, as you recall, if you are familiar with the Bible. Remember when the angel announced that his name would be Jesus, not Christ? He gained that title in later years.[6]

However, Jesus was himself a very, very, very high being and sent from this plane to embody The Christ. Now, we will also again explain that Jesus The Christ was the Son of God. Jesus The Christ.[7]

Now to explain and review what we have said about this at an earlier session:

The God Force is all there is and when the desire to make Itself

---

[6] Matt. 1: 20-21, 23 -- "...the angel of the Lord appeared unto him in a dream, saying, " Joseph, for that which is conceived in her is of the Holy Ghost. And she shall bring forth a son, and thou shalt call his name JESUS. Behold, a virgin shall be with child, and shall bring forth a son, and they shall call his name Emmanuel, which being interpreted is, God with us." — *NASB*

[7] Luke 2:11 — "For unto you is born this day in the City of David a Savior, which is Christ the Lord." — *NASB*

manifest was made, It, as both father-mother, gave birth to Itself as a Son. That Son was The Christ, the first impulse of life. Why son and not daughter? It was, in fact, both son and daughter. How could it be anything else? The male aspect or masculine aspect is what took form in Jesus, but not devoid of the feminine aspect. Both were present.

This is very detailed and we will keep it general tonight. Know that we could spend many sessions on each minute point, but tonight we wish to give you an overview of the whole. So we will continue.

Jesus was created sometime after the idea to bring the fuller light of The Christ onto this plane (celestial realm). He was created first on this plane, but even preceding that, much discussion was made among the great councils and commissions. During this period, those sitting at the highest level made the preparation by offering themselves as instruments for this work on your plane. Those who chose to prepare the way became the parents of the parents of Jesus.

In the Bible you only get part of the story. Much preparation was made long before Mary's birth. The wonderful beings who became the grandparents were the highest at this level of being. They sat as heads of very high commissions. They were revered, well loved and respected. They worked as teams on their planes, both sets of parents, meaning the parents of Joseph and Mary. Those who were here as the great heads of commissions functioned as guides for great masters.

We will begin with those who became Mary's parents.[8] They were very, very high teachers and guides. It was them whom great avatars stood before to be so titled. This is the esteem we had for them. They also worked with The Christ in designing the Universe. These were the highest among the highest.

And so, it was so desired by the God Force The Christ should thus be revealed with greater light upon the Earth. [This was] to help humankind feel less separation and mystery about their relationship as divine beings in Creation. It was they who decided to lead and prepare the way. Thus, they gave up their post here to enter your plane.

The same, too, happened with those who took the role as parents of Joseph.[9] They too sat on another

---

[8] "In the original transcription, the names were not correctly placed with the Councils. This is the proper assignment." —BEINGS OF THE CHRIST LIGHT, OCTOBER 14, 1997.
[9] Same as above

high commission governing the interaction of the celestial host and the spiritual guides aiding others such as yourselves, to name only a portion of their responsibilities. They, too, deemed it an honor to serve the God Force in this way and they relinquished their post to enter this plane. When born of humans, they were all born into the Essene community. This enabled them the guidance and lifestyle to promote their work.

It was not enough to impregnate a virgin. No, this required great preparation. It meant that a community of elders and wise ones had to be established to rear and train the parents-to-be. It could not be left to chance that Jesus was to be born into any good community. Being good was not enough. One must also have the consciousness to do the preparatory work. The Essenes were such a community. This was to be a long period of preparation, even before the parents of the parents were sent. The council—sending beings as humans onto your plane—spent several generations, sending them to lay a foundation for such a community. Then after some time they entered this plane one by one. However, unlike most, they (the parents of Joseph and Mary) entered with full awareness and purpose. Even through gestation and birth, they were with full awareness because of who they were here and their mission to prepare the parents of Jesus.

THE CREATION OF JESUS

So while this was occurring, thought was given to that which would receive The Christ in human form—the quality of such a child. Great rituals and ceremonies were held on this plane. And when it was decided that it was time, Jesus was thus created and done so in this manner on this plane:

Through these ceremonies and rituals, gifts were given, gifts that were the best of the highest here. They were not material gifts, but gifts of the being, of the heart, of the spirit, of awareness. Each high Being gave the best of itself to this Being; and thus, Jesus was created here. This was done even before the birth of Mary and Joseph or their parents.

We have generalized this event, because we want you to see the fuller picture.

So Jesus was thus created from the highest here, to be the highest there, for your plane. But even then, he was not prepared to receive The Christ; for he too had to do his inner work. This was his purpose in being born of woman, to be the example, not something unique.

What would you have gained had he been born with the full light of The Christ? Would you know or believe it was possible for you to do the same or greater. No! Some of you yet don't believe it! You would have been without hope as well as an example had The Christ revealed Itself in human form in any other way. Know beloveds, that The Christ spoke the truth when through Jesus It said, 'even greater things you can do.'

This Is the Real Meaning

As we enter this Holy season, celebrate the birth of Christ as it is now being born in you. It is not enough to celebrate the birth of the Baby Jesus. Celebrate the revelation of The Christ in you. The birth of Jesus means nothing if it does not inspire you to find the birth of Christ in you.

This is the real meaning of Christmas, not simply that Jesus was born to save you. He did not come

THE MEANING OF CHRISTMAS

simply to do that. That could have been done on this plane. Why bother with all the preparation simply to save you? Save you from what? And for what? To do what?

Let's say you are *saved*, as some of you identify yourselves. Now what? Are you living as divine beings or are you simply glad to be going to Heaven? It will not be much different from what you know here (on earth) if you are not willing to be more than you are now, while here. Being saved and going through death does not make you divine. It is a matter of choosing to do your own work.[10] You can do it now, or wait until later.

Many of you who are *saved* are still like the Prodigal Son[11]. You are saved from the pigsty, brought back into the father's house, but because your awareness has not changed, you live in the closet and do not enjoy the whole house.

You must do your work. This means doing more than obeying the Ten Commandments. The Commandments are for those who need them. When you are one with Divine Mind, you operate with

---

10 Luke 7:50 — "And He said to the woman, 'Your faith hath saved thee, go in peace.'" — *NASB*
[11] See: Luke 15:11-32

Divine Law in a very natural way.[12] No outside help is needed. You know that you know, for yourself. Living the Commandments is only a beginning. That is pre-school work! You must do your own inner work to do and be more. This means spending much time meditating and praying. This means thinking for yourself. This means listening to your own inner voice, to your own spiritual guides, to the voice of God within.

You won't find it in a book or in a sermon. Many may inspire you to do your work, but you must do it. By all means, continue to read and study, go to church and sit with your gurus, but do not stop there.

How is it that your preachers, your teachers, your gurus, your masters stay such clear open vessels? They continue to do their work. They cannot 'work' you. You must do it yourself. Even a great healer cannot keep you healed if your mind is not healed—even Jesus The Christ. Do you remember He admonished those He healed to go and sin no more? Meaning go, and do not commit the same error of

---

[12] Hebrews 8:10 — "...I will put My law into their minds, and I will write it on their heart; and I will be their God, and they shall be My people."- *AET*

THE MEANING OF CHRISTMAS

> thinking. The same error will bring back the same result.
> Do you see this?

"Yes. Yes," many people responded.

> Is this so, Rev. Dunn?

"Yes, yes, yes."

CHOOSING TO CELEBRATE THE CHRIST IN YOU

> So, now tell us, how will you choose to celebrate Christmas? Someone come speak.

Over the speakerphone, from Berkeley we hear, "Hi, it's Gitane. I know that Christ must be constant in my life in order for me to continue on my path."

> No! Christ *is* constant in your life. You must *choose* to have the awareness of Christ in your life.

"What I…"

> Do you see this, beloved?
> Stop here.

"Yes."

> Yes, what?

Yes, I see.

What is it you see?

"I see that Christ is constant in my life and that I am willing to be more than what I know I can be right now, by knowing this and meditating more."

Watch how you speak.

"Watch how I speak?"

Yes. You said that you are 'willing to be more than you know that you can be.' Is that what you mean, beloved?

"What?"

You said, 'you are willing to be more than you know that you can be.'

"Oh, no, no, no. That's not what I meant."

Then what is it you mean? Speak your word.

"I know..."

You see, beloved,—stop here. One of the things that we said is that you must be willing to think for yourself. Do not just spout out words.
You see, beloved?

THE MEANING OF CHRISTMAS

"Yes."

> You are responsible for your life.

"Yes," she agreed.

> Choose wisely what you say. Now, continue.

A few moments of silence passed as she formulated her thoughts.

More silence.

> Beloved?

"Yes?"

> Yes, continue. Are you taking time to think?

"I'm taking time to think."

> Very good. Would you like to do this and then come back?

"Yes!" she answered in a way that sounded as if she was glad to be spared from answering right then. "That would be great! Thank you," she said sounding relieved.

> Very good.
> Who else?

"Yes," said a man visiting for the first time. "I always go outside to look for something, but it's inside. I know that inside is where I find what's blocking me. I feel the peace inside. It feels good inside, but then I get diverted off into some other direction and I don't focus and I don't know what … my ego, whatever you want to call it, just draws me away from the truth. I just surrender to that and then really have to keep the faith there."

> Yes, yes, yes. Let us look at one point. Did you say that ego diverts you from being within?

"Right."

> Let us have a clearer understanding about this. Let us make this simple. It is not the ego. Let us just say it is fear.

"Very good. Fear that I'm not enough…"

> Yes, yes.

"…and fear that what's beautiful in front of me needs to be fixed and just can't be accepted the way it is," he said.

> Nothing needs to be accepted the way it is.

"I don't understand."

THE MEANING OF CHRISTMAS

> Not unless you *choose* to accept it and that is all right, but it does not need to be. We will ask you to come again before we go too deeply into this. This is back to some of our basic lessons.

The Beings continued with a question.

> Beloved one, this Christmas, you will celebrate The Christ within you?

"Yes. I feel alone....Do I go into detail about personal things that have happened or do I make it simple?" Hearing himself, he knew he already had the answer and said, "Keep it simple."

> Tonight lets keep it simple.
> Is there something pressing you want to share? We do not want to hear stories just to hear stories.

"This is the first time I've been—not been in a relationship with a family for Christmas in 18 years and I was feeling sad about that."

> Is this because you've moved away?

"No, they've moved away and I broke off a relationship or we changed form," he answered. "Anyhow, I was in self pity about that and I forgot what Christmas is all about. It isn't about Jingle Bells, and trees. It's about Jesus and Christ and inside of me…"

> Yes, yes.

"And that Christ being born inside of me, like you said. And that's a beautiful way to see Christmas. That is the essence of it. So, it's nice."

> Thank you, beloved.

"Thank you."

> We do want to say to each of you, yes, do celebrate the birth of the Baby Jesus, but do not celebrate this birth alone, because when you celebrate only the birth of Jesus you separate 'That' from yourself. Do you see this?

"Yes. Yes," those listening answered

> Yes, Jesus is to be revered and honored. Celebrate the birth of Jesus as an example to you, but along with that celebrate the birth of The Christ within you.
>
> So who else would like to share with us how they would like to celebrate Christmas?

Again from the Bay Area, over the speakerphone, we hear a voice. "This is Deborah."

THE MEANING OF CHRISTMAS

> Yes, Deborah.

"I also have a tendency to get caught up with expectations of the season and being around family. I'm just coming back. I've been fluctuating in and out, distracting myself from being quiet and I'm just now coming back to celebrate the wonder of myself."

> Very good, very good.

"I've been spending some time with that and allowing whatever is to happen, to happen and not really schedule events, but just receive what's going to come to me.

"I guess that is it," she concluded.

> Whether you celebrate with family or alone, remember The Christ within you. We are not suggesting that you so celebrate The Christ within you, that you separate yourself from your family and loved ones. No. This is not necessary. This is a state of awareness.

"But, I am separate from my family physically," Deborah explained. "And Christmas on the West Coast seems much different from Christmas on the East Coast. I have a tendency to…it's not as real to me here because of all of the externals…there's not the snow, not the family. So now it's becoming an opportunity for me to create a new type of tradition for myself."

> Very good.

"Thank you."

> Yes, Thank you, beloved. Who is next?

"This is Bruce.

"Yes, I'm very grateful for what I'm hearing and for being in the presence of the Beings this evening. My gratitude has to do with my past Christmases—not only the [spiritual] work that I have been doing, but as a child living abroad in a country celebrating Christmas a great deal, as well as here. I've always felt very lonely and depressed at Christmas time, not being in contact with what was being celebrated and not understanding it at all.

"Tonight, with what I am hearing, I now understand it and it is....I really have a great deal of gratitude for this information that I am receiving. Along with the work that I've been doing, I received a confirmation in what I've been hearing inwardly about the work that I have done to move forward. I realize that 'the work' is the way to move forward. I'm patting myself on the back for the work that I've done because this is my salvation. I'm very grateful to be here."

> Very good, beloved. Anyone else?

"Yes, S.H.," the woman said, identifying herself to the people listening via telephone from Berkeley.

THE MEANING OF CHRISTMAS

Yes, beloved.

"Yes, I am rejoicing" she said holding back her emotions. "I am rejoicing in that I no longer have to hold on to the memories, the bad memories, the confusion associated with, not only with my family, associated with the commercialism that is practiced in this country. And I'm celebrating knowing and confirming that the *work* is the way for me and I am worth celebrating."

Yes, yes, yes, yes, yes!

"Hallelujah!" she shouted.

Yes, yes, yes, beloved. Thank you.

"Thank you."

"This is Dee. I would like to come forward," said the next speaker.

Yes, please come forward, beloved.

She took a few moments as she fought back tears.

Breathe, beloved. Take your time.

"I made that commitment to walk through the door…it didn't matter. I made that commitment…I know the essence of that Christ experience in me, clear in each moment. Of all the teachings I've been brought up with, my experience in various things…

"A short background: On Sunday," she explained. "I went to my mother's church and I felt—this past Sunday—I recommitted myself and I want to be baptized again. This is what I want to do. This is what I want to do. I'm not here to showboat or anything. I need this. I needed to go home."

Yes, yes, yes.

"I was raised Baptist. I experienced growth in TM (Transcendental Meditation). I experienced study in Islam. I saw that making this commitment back to home—the church of my mother's church, my daughter's church—that I was going to be in that commitment. Because the study that I am doing, moment by moment, is keeping me really focused on that Christ consciousness growing in me. I have to feel seated in that, feel it every moment and feel comfortable without having to defend it. That's how I know I plan to celebrate Christmas.

"I find myself feeling much love and all of a sudden a thought goes into something very gross. Then I say, 'Whoa! I have to keep this [Christ consciousness].'— I am just making sure there is no strain and allowing myself to make the mistakes. I just keep loving me. I'm finished. This is a lot of work and I'm enjoying it, too."

Remember [that whether] at the church or the mosque, you must

THE MEANING OF CHRISTMAS

"Remain your own authority on the voice of God within you."

know God for yourself. Neither the minister nor the imam can give it to you. They can lead you to it, but you must find it, pick it up, and receive it yourself. Remain your own authority on the voice of God within [you]. Do not make the minister your God. He does not want that burden. He wants only to lead you to God—not to become your God. This is your work, not his responsibility.

Now we thank you, beloved one, for your love and work.

"Thank you. Thank you for that light," Dee answered.

Who is next? Anyone else, someone in the Bay Area?

"K. is coming," is heard over the speakerphone.

Yes, K?

"I'm excited for the first time—probably in twenty years—about Christmas."

"Very good, beloved."

"I use to—in the past, my family would get together, fight and get drunk and yell at each other and go away. But this year, my sister in Florida and her six sons and daughters went in together and got me an Amtrak ticket to Florida...."

"Very good, beloved."

"...because they are ready to hear from me and how I've turned my life around. I've been given an opportunity to show tradition," she said speaking of her Native American heritage, "and share my love with my nieces and nephews."

Yes.

"I'm very excited. I'm very excited that I have another opportunity to share with someone that they have everything they need to turn their lives around...."

Yes.

"...and walk in a good way. I'm very excited! And, also on my returning, I have an opportunity to do a performance with some women in San Francisco. And the theme is about incest survivors who have turned their lives around."

Very good, very good.

"So, I'm really excited about my life."

As a survivor, do you see yourself as a victim?

"No," she said.

Very good! Very good! Very good!

THE MEANING OF CHRISTMAS

"Not at all," she continued. "I see it as an opportunity to teach people that life's lessons are there for a purpose."

> Yes, yes, yes. Very good, beloved.

"So, I'm feeling really grateful," she said.

> Yes, yes, beloved. We bless you, beloved one.

"Thank you," she said.

> Yes and who is next here?

"B. T.," answered the man. "Yes. The question is how do I celebrate Christmas?" he said. "Well, I began to notice that the same spirit that was in Jesus is also in me and that spirit is the Father. So, in celebration of Christmas, I will look no further than to go within myself. I relinquish myself. I just listen to His advice and this will be done through meditation and prayer. I wish that His grace will flow through me and by me, and to all those who ask to receive the light. So, that is my wish for Christmas."

> Very good, very good, very good, very good. You have grown greatly, beloved one. Very good, very good, very good.
>
> Does anyone else care to share?

Over the speakerphone we hear, "Yes, this is P. M."

> Yes, beloved.

"I just wanted to come forward and give thanks…"

> Yes, beloved one.

She continued, "…for the opportunity to serve The Christ in this year—it has been a very blessed year—and for this opportunity to be born again in The Christ, consciously. I just wanted to thank you for coming to be with us. Thank you," she said.

> Thank you, precious daughter.
> Who is next?

"Thank you, is the first thing I want to say to the Beings of the Christ Light. This is Pamela?"

> Yes, beloved.

"I feel so full and I feel so expectant, like giving birth," Pamela continued. "This Christmas will be the first true Christmas I've ever known. I already feel the cycles of The Christ consciousness coming to full term within me and I will always know this to be the first full birth of The Christ consciousness within me. So, I am now giving birth to the highest meaning of Christmas that I have always wondered about. Even in this very moment, I am so full of love for all the light that is within this room from all of the people that I love. I love each and every person in this room—and that love is marrying light.

"I don't see it as a graduation," she continued, "but a true birth, a true first moment, a true first breath, a true first consciousness. And so, all I can say is thank you for this moment."

> Beloved one…

The Beings began their response to her and then included the others.

> …and each of you who are feeling the fullness—thank you for coming.
> Is someone coming next?

They stopped and then turned their attention to the woman who took time to think from earlier in the evening. They called for her.

> Gitane?

"Yes," answered the woman over the speakerphone.

> Yes, beloved one.

"Okay. Let me begin by saying I am eternally grateful for this opportunity to have been in the Presence, and to have witnessed myself grow with the love that Christ and you all have allowed me by having this opportunity since June.

She continued, "How will I celebrate Christmas in my life now that I know the real meaning of Christmas? As I am more aware of my mind and my thoughts, choosing to love more, is one way. I will celebrate The Christ within me as I choose more love—love and light…"

> Very good.

"I intend to celebrate Christmas with everyone and see The Christ in them, as well as myself.…"

> Good. Very good.

"…and allow myself the time and the love to process, and allow my truth to be expressed in every area of my life. Learning to humble myself and come from my own authority in words, thoughts and actions; to take full responsibility for my choices. This is truly the birth of The Christ in me. This is a full celebration of my intention. I am grateful to myself, my soul for choosing my path, and grateful to the people who are in front of me—to give me the opportunity to grow and benefit from my experience.

"Thank you," she gratefully concluded.

> Good work, beloved, good work. Very good, very good. Thank you, beloved.
> Yes, someone else is here?

"Yes," answered one woman.

THE MEANING OF CHRISTMAS

Yes. Thank you, beloved.

"This is Vrindavana. There are so many things that I heard tonight that I would like to address but cannot address them all. The statements that the Beings have given us to read before we go to bed and when we wake up in the morning," she said referring to a previous session. "The perception of those in my mind and the experience of them in my life, are two different things."

Does someone have those words to share with the others?

"I have them," Cynthia, one of the participants said, holding her notes. She began reading the instructions. "The affirmations are,

Read upon awaking in the morning and at night before retiring:

I am whole and complete.
I am free now.
I can see now.
As I choose to see, I am one with Creation.
I live in the eternal now.
I am free, I am clear, I am light, I am love.'"

The Light Beings explained:

This was along with some exercises that we have been using to guide those who have been attending, helping them to practice seeing what we see. This is all part of the process of learning to trust what

> you know. This is part of our work with you.
>
> Now this is a simple affirmation, but the words are not the power. It is the choice of accepting the truth of your words which is pure awareness of yourself as being born as a divine being. We want you to understand that repetition of an affirmation has some merit, but limited. It is the awareness of the truth behind the words. This may be through the repetition, if you —over a period—open to the truth or by simply choosing, in an instant, the truth behind the words.

Again, the Beings addressed Vrindavana.

> Now, beloved one, please continue.

"What I found is that I really do know," she continued. "But when I say I don't know, it is that I choose not to know."

> Yes, yes, yes.

"Also," she continued, "what I found, is that the freedom in my choices…and something I heard the Light Beings repeat over and over—and this week it was, like, bombarded in me—is that my words, how I speak my words, and the choices I make for my words,

THE MEANING OF CHRISTMAS

are very important because that's what I'm building...for myself...."

Yes, yes.

"...And what it makes me do when—I really look at choosing my words—is that it makes me be the master and co-creator of my own experience."

Yes, yes, yes. Very good, very good.

"...And what I'm learning is to implement that on the level of the impulse of the desire.

Yes, very good.

"That's the level I'm striving for right now...."

"Very good! Very good! VERY GOOD! The Creation process! Very good!

"...Yes! And I'm really teaching myself how to be my master in my life and I'm showing this to myself. Sometimes I'm getting frustrated...to get it, to maintain it and to keep it, but I'm learning this.

She concluded, "Everyone have happy holidays."

Thank you, beloved. One more here and then we will end.

"This is TarunKrishna. I have at this moment such profound reverence and respect for all of the teachers in this lifetime that have guided me to this moment, guided us to this moment. And I like to especially thank the Supreme Lord, sweet Lord, sweet Lord for His great mercy. I would like to thank my mother for being my second guru in this lifetime and I'd like to send out love to her for her sweetness, unconditional love and great sacrifice."

He continued, "Lord, a special thanks for allowing me to come out of the analytical and into the heart—and to contain it all, and to contain it all. A special thanks for my peers, all of you wonderful people who also have been important gurus for my process and your process. I feel very androgynous, no gender tonight. Spirit tonight. I'm going to work real hard this year—for the rest of my life—to stay in this fullness, to stay in this unconditional love that belongs to me, that's my legacy. It is a legacy from the lord, The Christ Love. Thank you, all of my sisters and brothers, thank you."

We thank you for this year you have allowed us to be with you. We thank you for the time you have taken from your schedules to sit with us. We know that this has often been difficult for some. We also thank you for serving as our emissary on our behalf in giving to our beloved instrument.

Thank you for your growth and the steps you have been willing to take. You are now well on your way to achieving mastery. You are moving beyond intellectual

THE MEANING OF CHRISTMAS

> "Take nothing as truth simply because we have said it."

understanding to being the thing Itself. It is not due to us, but your own work. We cannot do it for you.

Take nothing as truth simply because we have said it. You must know for yourselves, within yourselves. What we see, you can see. What we are, you are. You are our peers, for you all are workers in the Light of The Christ. This is not because we say so, but because you chose to be such. This is your life, your choice. You now know freedom in being your own authority. You now know yourselves as co-creators of your lives. Do not forget, forgetting is a choice.

Now, beloved ones, we go to be with The Christ in our own High Holy celebration. We will be gone for a period of time and perhaps back before the end of the year. While away we will assist others on this side in their Ascension. We will also help The Christ in these celebrations. It is a most joyous time.

We wish for you the same joy as you celebrate. Now, we do not bestow such joyous celebrations upon you. That is in your own making.

Thank you, beloved ones. And, so it is.

Live your lives in freedom. Live your lives in peace. Live your lives in joy. Live your lives in love. Live your lives in the light.

Good Bye.

Afterword

On

Spiritual Mastery

Dear Reader,

Now that you have arrived at this point, the Beloved Beings of the Christ Light requested that I offer suggestions that may further assist you with this work. Many of the people that were present when this story was told had an advantage that others did not have. They were fortunate that they first had the benefit of direct exposure to the Beings' reoccurring themes on obtaining spiritual mastery. This happened through several weeks to months of attendance at weekly sessions.

To contribute to you in a similar way, I will bring to your attention the underlying themes of spiritual mastery recorded in this book. If you find yourself once again reading this work, these will be more evident to you. You will also be introduced to new excerpts from sessions not included here. This supplemental material will reinforce what you have read.

I begin by reminding you that their mission is...

THE MEANING OF CHRISTMAS

> ...to awaken you to your enlightenment... to assist you in recognizing the divinity that is yours...[1]

If you feel that this is a call to your heart, yet wonder what is the next step that you must take toward embodying the fullness of your chosen spiritual/religious path, then it is suggested that you remember the instructions given in the "PROLOGUE" section, "AWAKENED BY THE LIGHT":

> You must listen to your heart and mind. You will know what you need to know and to do soon. Trust and allow God to work through you.[2]

Along with being reminded of the basic points for achieving spiritual mastery, the people in attendance at those sessions were also blessed to receive the Light Beings' direct guidance. Week after week, we were assisted in expanding our ability to listen and follow the inner guidance of the Divine Teacher. We were led to see how closely our spiritual understanding matched our commitment to living these spiritual truths. When we sought answers, the Beings helped us to use our discernment to more clearly recognize and listen to the divine inner voice. This guidance strengthened our union with God.

---

[1] See: p. 33
[2] See: p. 25

AFTERWORD ❖ Spiritual Mastery

Awareness of the following themes may be helpful to you whether your faith is grounded in a strong religious conviction, if any kind of spiritual development is new to you, or if you are a long-time seeker on a spiritual path. In some instances where those themes are discussed below, there will only be references made to them. It will be of benefit to you to review the pages as you see them footnoted.

Choice and Co-creation

Your chosen way to know God will be better served as you gain greater understanding of the Beings' views on "choice" and the "co-creation process" as they relate to your own spiritual mastery. It is how "the God Force expressed Itself as Creation and that is how you find the results you now experience in your life."[3]

This understanding brings us closer to our own divinity and to the significance of the inner celebration of The Christ. You may wish to again look at the basic points that are covered in the section of the "Prologue" entitled "Light Sessions."[4]

Your Own Authority

You may recall that throughout the book the Beings cited the importance of trusting our own authority. One such passage read:

---
[3] See: p. 36
[4] See: pp. 34–45

THE MEANING OF CHRISTMAS

> Remain your own authority on the voice of God within [you]. Do not make the minister your God. He does not want that burden. He wants only to lead you to God—not to become your God. This is your work, not his responsibility.[5]

To further assist you, you might benefit from reading excerpts from a session held in November of 1994, the year that the Beings of the Christ Light first told us *THE MEANING OF CHRISTMAS*.

In this session the Beings again spoke on authority. They began that session by announcing, "Now we will be going into a new phase. This is to speed up the process of mastery."[6] They later went on to say that this is the time to "take full authority, ...To have control of your thinking, to control it in a way that will benefit you as you so desire."[7]

In this session the following instructions were given on living in your authority. As you read, keep in mind the Beings' views on the themes of choice and co-creation:

> 1. When making a decision [you must] be certain of what you want. We will explain. You must be clear on your intent. Is it simply to have some curiosity fulfilled or is it to have concrete change? This is important, especially in the beginning.

---

[5] See: p. 134
[6] November 11, 1994
[7] Same as above.

> Now we want to further elaborate on this point. You must always think as a co-creator from this time forward. Know and accept who you are as a spiritual being.
>
> Now we will further elaborate. This is vital in the creation process. You must act as a co-creator with God. Not as one who waits upon the "will of God."[8] You must act as the God Force Itself incarnate in you. This is key.

Remember that the Beings would often make such statements to encourage our growth and reflection upon the truth in our lives. Is the "will of God" a living presence operating through us or is it confined to being a familiar intellectual spiritual idea in our lives?[9]

> 2. This is the next step or principle to understand: You must not allow doubt to enter your mind. State your intention. State your purpose and let it be.
>
> No doubt, no doubt, no doubt.
>
> Now this is your birthright to demand of the universe your wants. The universe is neutral and its function is to respond to the demand of Divine Mind. You are one with

---

[8] Ephesians 6:7 — "Not with eyeservice, as hypocrites, but as the servants of Christ, doing the will of God from the heart. And serve well with your whole soul, with love, as to our Lord, and not to men.—*AET*

[9] Romans 12:2 — "Do not imitate the way of this world, but be transformed by the renewing of your minds, that you may discern what is that good and acceptable and perfect will of God." — *AET*

THE MEANING OF CHRISTMAS

Divine Mind. You and the Father are one. You are here to be the embassy for Pure Spirit. Pure Spirit resides within you. This is your function as a spiritual being.

3. We also want you to think big. Think without limitations. Think with an expansive heart and mind. Think, as you are inspired. Think as you feel from deep within. Step out boldly. Claim your wants boldly, but do not impose your wants upon others.

4. You must be vigilant in thought. Be very clear on your intent to always bring forth the higher good. In this regard, you must only demand for others their highest good, not what you [may] feel is best [for them]. This is critical to stay in harmony with Divine Law. You are responsible even for your prayers and their outcome.[10] This is a must. You must live by this or suffer the consequences, which you will create for yourself.

5. No one is to use this authority for evil, to hurt or harm anything in the universe. Use your authority only for good.

6. Be of good cheer. Be optimistic. Be expectant of only good.

7. Do not make this a game, but a way of life.

8. No more fear, ever.

9. Live in the Truth of your Divinity.

---

[10] Matthew 21:22 — "And everything that you will ask in prayer believing, you shall receive —*AET*

10. Do it now.

In reference to point number 4, it may be useful for you to review on page 27 beginning with the quote by the Beings through the end of that section on page 28 in the "PROLOGUE • AWAKENED BY THE LIGHT." We are reminded that our words of faith do not always match our thoughts and feelings. Sometimes what we call our faith must grow to meet our words. This includes our prayer work, as well. You'll see this same point expressed in other ways throughout the book.

TRUSTING YOUR INNER GUIDANCE

Later in that same session, the beloved Beings of the Christ Light went on to give further guidance that served as a reminder. You may recall reading a similar offering in the "PROLOGUE • LIGHT SESSIONS."[11] This may be useful as you move toward greater understanding. The Beings offered "our instruction for learning how to trust your inner guidance."

1. Listen.
2. Listen.
3. Listen.
4. Don't doubt.
5. Don't doubt.
6. Don't doubt.
7. Listen more.
8. Listen again.
9. Respond.

---

[11] See: p. 43

10. Make yourself a full participant in the experience.
11. Begin now.
12. Take it one step at a time.
13. Be patient and loving with yourself.
14. Don't criticize yourself—ever.
15. Love yourself.
16. Trust that you always know what to do and when to do it.
17. Do not wonder 'how', simply be clear on your intent to commune.
18. Never ask, 'Why me?"
19. Accept your divine authority.

They also offered a cautionary point just before sharing these points on trusting your inner guidance. This is particularly important for those who become enamored with their ability to communicate with unseen forces. Because there is communication it does not mean that such communication is of the Light, as we read in their words:

> Demand only that that which is of The Christ make itself known to you. Once the door is opened . . . don't be afraid to ask who it is. Always ask. You have a right to know. You are the authority of your lives. Honor yourself.
>
> Do not become a puppet to anything, even to The Christ. The Christ loves you as a full participant of your own volition.

UNDERSTAND WHO YOU ARE

The divine nature of our lives is another point that the Beloved Beings frequently sought to help us understand.

> We wish to help each of you achieve mastery over your lives; each of you to know yourselves as co-creators. This is who you truly are. You create your life, as you desire. God Force has already given this gift to you.[12]

That is a point that was made in almost all of their sessions. To provide greater clarity on this point, I've added here an excerpt that may assist you from another session.[13] I feel it is quite fitting because it is from the session that immediately preceded the Christmas message.

> We want you to understand who you are. You are not bound by circumstance or conditions. You are free, loving beings of creation. You must take this in the fullness of what we say. We are not simply stating poetic phrases for your entertainment. What we say is the truth of the Creation. You are indeed manifestations of the Divine. Recognize yourself as such and you

---

[12] See: p. 34
[13] General Session December 2, 1994

THE MEANING OF CHRISTMAS

will receive such help from the Celestial Realms. So, as you know and live as you truly are, your life will unfold in this way.

We are glad that you are listening and honoring yourself more and more. You are finding it more and more difficult to use the old thought patterns.

Is this so? Does that not seem to be quite uncomfortable and heavy?

So, you are shedding this old cloak. When you try to step back into this old garment you find it no longer fits. So, now only wear your right garment, your garment of Light. This means wear love instead of fear. Wear trust instead of doubt. Wear peace and not confusion.

You have shopped on a new boulevard. Your address is now changed. The old neighborhood no longer suits you. Only visit it to clean it and bring Light, but do not move back. Invite your old neighbors to more often visit you so they may have the vision of what is possible. Do not feel guilt because you are moving on. If you decide to stay where you are, then fine. But know that you can always remodel. So, bring where you are up to the highest. Do not settle for the routine because that is what you see around you. No. You be the Light.

> This applies as a metaphor for conscious growth as well as your actual physical life.
>
> Do you understand?

CLOSING THOUGHTS FROM THE BEINGS OF THE CHRIST LIGHT

In their closing statement that follows, you are given a gift that we did not receive during the three years of their weekly public sessions. You are given the gift of their identity.

During that period of their public sessions, the Beings continued to encourage us individually to trust the way in which God guides us, to trust what we sense, feel, and know for ourselves. They continued to hold to their statement, "Take nothing as truth simply because we have said it." This included knowing them or about them. During that three year period the comments that they made about themselves did not go much beyond what you read near the beginning[14] of the book and in later chapters as they told this Christmas story.[15]

A few days before holding the first of these three years of public sessions where I served as the instrument for these Beings of Light, they told me their reason for not speaking much about their identity.

> Now we are going to tell you more about us.

---

[14] See: p. 5
[15] See: p. 79

> We are also of the light, as Beings of the Light. Now we have a mission, as directed by The Christ, to find people like you to work with and through[16] to help raise consciousness and the spiritual nature of humans on earth.
>
> Now, we will begin to make ourselves known to many others.
>
> You must not tell this to others, yet.
>
> They must discover their own contact themselves. You must not do anything to put ideas into their head. Just tell them to simply trust and allow Spirit to work through them. And so it is. Amen.
>
> They will begin to have deeper trust and faith. And so it is. Amen.[17]

If they are of God and sent to us by The Christ then this we must know for ourselves. Not because they have said it is so. We learn to discern the truth as the Presence of God abides in us and we consciously choose to abide in It.[18]

It was not until the year 2001 when we once again assembled together in observation of Easter that they identified themselves in this same way that you will soon read in their statement to you. The time had come for them to clearly make it known that they are

---

[16] I believe that here they speak generally of spiritual awaking, rather than the specific way that these Light Beings give expression through me.
[17] To Mpingo: January 4, 1994
[18] 1 Corinthians 2:10, 14 — "but God has revealed it to us by his Spirit. ...because they are spiritually discerned. *New International Version (NIV)*

indeed directed by God and that their purpose is much greater than our personal spiritual unfoldment.

They now come forward in this way because of the urgency of the times. You have probably sensed or felt the divine urge to embody the highest teachings that have served your life. It seems that these days there is an urgent call to people who now serve God or want to serve God and stand as beacons of light in these times and times soon to come.

It is not my intention to be evasive. I seriously considered quoting what they will now say to you about themselves earlier in this Afterword. Whether I would have said it earlier or left it for you to read directly from the Beings, you must judge this for yourself. I do not ask or suggest you believe it. Quite frankly, I believe that what is most important is that the wisdom of the Beings of the Christ Light assists you in your personal walk with God. Whoever or from wherever they come, I am thankful that they always seek to turn us—not to them but—to God.

To you in closing, dear friend, the Beloved Ones say the following.

> You are now invited to once again review what you have read. This time as you read, discuss with others what you have been reminded of about yourself.

THE MEANING OF CHRISTMAS

Now friend, we will also suggest that as you read the section on "The Story" that you not look too much to historical detail, but rather look at the main points about divine law that you may incorporate into your own life. As you do this, you will find new insight. What you have read here will open doors to your own personal celebration of the Christ within you.

Remember, beloved one, you were made in our image and likeness.[19] We are the ones that spoke, that you have read of in Genesis 1:26. Know your divine nature, beloved reader. We are to assist.

Those of you who live a prayerful life already know this divine presence. We say to you, celebrate this. Celebrate the divinity that is within you as you celebrate the blessed birth of the Blessed Jesus who was sent to redeem the world. Celebrate the divinity that you were given at birth. Remember, beloved reader, it is enough to celebrate the fact that God created you.

---

[19] Genesis 1:26 — "Then God said, 'Let Us make man in Our image, according to Our likeness'…" — *NAS*

AFTERWORD ❖ SPIRITUAL MASTERY

Go deeper. Beloved friend, go deeper into the meaning of Christmas. Do you really think you are only to celebrate the Birth of Jesus? You who walk a spiritual and/or religious path have more to celebrate than this expression of God, known as Jesus.

Beloved friend, remember who you are.

—*Beings of the Christ Light*

Acknowledgements

I thank the beloved Beings of the Christ Light for sharing their love, light, wisdom and guidance.

I am thankful for each person that attended the sessions and shared this experience with me.

I thank Christopher Harper for all that he has done to bring the work of the Beings of The Christ Light the public. Included with him are three others, IfeTayo Theresa Bonner-Payne, R. Chinelo Haney, and Sibongile West, who have all remained steadfast with their support and in holding the vision for this and future publications.

Thank you Denise David for the loving editorial guidance that you so generously gave to this project.

I am greatly appreciative of the great care Isabela Harper gave to this project.

Thanks to all who generously provided support or offered their comments and corrections after reading my original photocopy version of the book or the draft of this text: Sananda Ananda, Bruce Bryant, Mawiyah Clayborne, Baadia Daaood, Myrna Campbell, Deborah Carvalho, Jane Derenne, The Dobbins, Molly Doty, Ananda Edmonds, Cedrick Estridge, Tsehai Esseibea Farrell, Michael and Denise Harrington; Diane Houston, Pamela Jones, Bob Kealing, Anthony Lloyd, Aliah MaJon, Dee Monroe, Adowa Nyamekye, Cordell Richardson, Angela Sanchez, and Kakwasi Somadhi.

Thank you Rev. Thomas Brown of Indianapolis, Indiana for your understanding and encouragement.

Also, a very special thanks to those who wish to remain anonymous.

"Live your lives in freedom
Live your lives in peace.
Live your lives in joy.
Live your lives in love.
Live your lives in the light."

—Beings of the Christ Light